BRIDGING GRADES

1&2

Summer
Big Fun Workbook

For information about permission to reproduce selections from this book for
an entire school or school district, please contact permissions@highlights.com.

Published by Highlights Learning • 815 Church Street • Honesdale, Pennsylvania 18431
ISBN: 978-1-68437-290-4
Mfg. 04/2023
Printed in Mattoon, IL, USA
First edition
10 9 8 7 6 5

For assistance in the preparation of this book, the editors would like to thank:
Vanessa Maldonado, MSEd; MS Literacy Ed. K–12; Reading/LA Consultant Cert.; K–5 Literacy Instructional Coach
Kristin Ward, MS Curriculum, Instruction, and Assessment; K–5 Mathematics Instructional Coach
Jump Start Press, Inc.

Your child's summer learning adventure starts here!

This book is divided into eight chapters, each designed to bridge first and second grade and give your child practice in a variety of curriculum areas all summer long.

Tips for using this book with your child:

1 Find the right time.
Whenever possible, start new activities in the morning or following a snack or meal—any time she is well fed and rested.

2 Let your child take the lead.
If your child is eager to keep going, encourage him to do so, but don't pressure him to complete a certain number of pages or even finish an activity.

3 Take it with you.
Learning can happen anywhere. Bring this book with you during your summertime travels for learn-on-the-go fun in the car, on a plane, or even in the backyard.

4 Pour on the praise.
When your child works hard on an activity, acknowledge her efforts enthusiastically. She'll love that you're excited, and she'll be happy about her efforts and actions.

5 Join the fun.
At the end of each chapter is a bonus activity, such as a recipe, craft, or science project. You can also extend the learning by playing math games—using dominoes, dice, or a deck of cards—and by encouraging your child to compare prices at stores and read signs when you go for a walk.

and Yes to Big Fun!

As your child journeys through the book, she can track her progress by placing stickers on the **Summer Big Fun Adventure Poster**.

Here's how:

1 Remove the poster from the back of the book and unfold it. Hang it up or place it on a flat surface.

2 To advance along the path, your child will complete the activities in a chapter of the book.

3 When your child has completed a chapter, he will place that chapter's sticker from the sticker sheet on the correct signpost on the poster.

4 Once your child has placed all eight signpost stickers, she has completed her journey and earned her Achievement Certificate.

BONUS FUN!

The colorful nature walk poster is also a Hidden Pictures® puzzle! It is hiding 20 magnifying glasses for your child to find.

 Each time your child finishes a chapter, add a sticker!

Place a sun sticker on each hidden magnifying glass!

 Use the emoji stickers to mark favorite activities in the book!

Contents

Each chapter covers a variety of subjects, so that kids will get practice in different curriculum areas throughout the summer to help prevent learning loss and bridge the gap between first and second grades.

Don't forget!

Your Hidden Pictures poster and stickers are at the back of this book!

CHAPTER 1

ABC Warm-Up

Buzzy is heading home to her hive. She can travel only in alphabetical order. Trace all the uppercase and lowercase letters to help her buzz back home.

A Day at the Park

Look at this picture, then answer the counting questions on the next page.

What are your favorite things to do at a park?

High-Frequency Words: Number Words

Use a capital letter at the beginning of a sentence.

Write the correct number word to complete each sentence.

> one   two   three
> four   five   eight   twelve

I see _____ kids playing in the park.

_____ of the kids are wearing

red hats or helmets.

_____ are wearing yellow hats.

_____ bees are buzzing around.

I see _____ baseball gloves.

I also see _____ birds and

_____ dog.

Bird Watching

Skip count by 5's. Fill in the missing numbers from 0 to 120.

0				20
		35		45
		60	65	
	80			95
	105			120

Can you find the **12** objects in this Hidden Pictures® puzzle?

How many birds do you see?

sock

necktie

frying pan

pear

whale

paintbrush

pineapple

trophy

teacup

open book

stopwatch

glove

Missing Letters

Write the missing letter in each word using the consonant **m**, **s**, or **c**.

 __oose

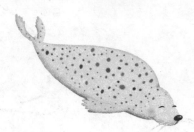 __eal

 broo__

 __ar

 __un

 __ake

 __oup

 __ilk

 __oin

Food Groups

Which group has the most food items?

Count and circle **10** foods in each group. Then count the extra ones. Fill in the chart to tell how many tens and ones are in the group. We did one to get you started.

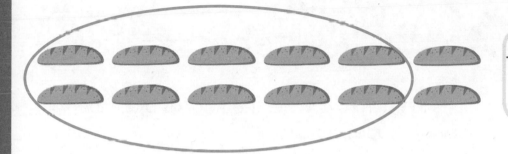

Tens	Ones
1	2

Tens	Ones

Tens	Ones

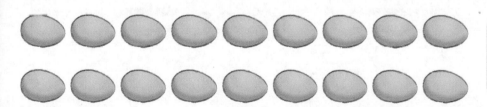

Tens	Ones

Tens	Ones

Bunches of Ten

Why aren't grapes ever lonely?
Because they come in bunches!

Each bunch of grapes below has 10 grapes.
You can think of each bunch as a **ten**.

 = [3] tens = [30]

Count the bunches of grapes in each row. Write the total as a number of tens and as the total number of grapes.

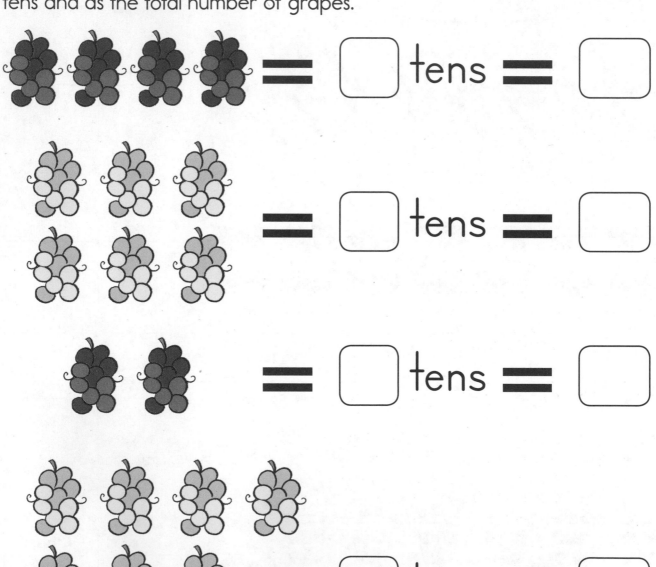

= [ ] tens = [ ]

= [ ] tens = [ ]

= [ ] tens = [ ]

= [ ] tens = [ ]

Party Fun

Rewrite these statements about the party to make them correct. Use an uppercase letter at the beginning and a period at the end of each statement.

the dog is wearing a hat

_____

the cake has seven candles

_____

a boy is laughing

_____

a girl waits for cake

_____

Now write your own statement about the party.

_____

_____

You can use a number line to **add**. Start with the first number. Then count on the second number to find the sum.

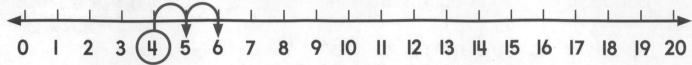

| 0 | 1 | 2 | 3 | 4 | 5 | 6 | 7 | 8 | 9 | 10 | 11 | 12 | 13 | 14 | 15 | 16 | 17 | 18 | 19 | 20 |

$$4 + 2 = 6$$

Find the sums. Use the number line to help you. Then find each sum in the code box. Write the letters that match the sums to solve the riddle. We did one to get you started.

What did the glove say to the baseball?

" $\underline{C}$ $\underline{}$ $\underline{}$ $\underline{}$ $\underline{}$

$13 + 7 = \boxed{20}$ $7 + 8 = \boxed{}$ $2 + 10 = \boxed{}$ $20 + 0 = \boxed{}$ $0 + 3 = \boxed{}$

$\underline{}$ $\underline{}$ $\underline{}$

$8 + 9 = \boxed{}$ $3 + 5 = \boxed{}$ $5 + 11 = \boxed{}$

$\underline{}$ $\underline{}$ $\underline{}$ $\underline{}$ $\underline{}$!"

$12 + 1 = \boxed{}$ $6 + 9 = \boxed{}$ $2 + 10 = \boxed{}$ $1 + 4 = \boxed{}$ $5 + 5 = \boxed{}$

CODE BOX				
3 = H	8 = O	12 = T	15 = A	17 = Y
5 = E	10 = R	13 = L	16 = U	20 = C

You can use a number line to **subtract**. Start with the first number. Then count back the second number to find the difference.

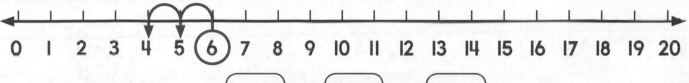

$$6 - 2 = 4$$

Find the differences. Use the number line to help you. Then find each difference in the code box. Write the letters that match to solve the riddle.

When do monkeys play baseball?

____ ____ ____ ____

$8 - 8 = \boxed{}$ $14 - 8 = \boxed{}$ $2 - 1 = \boxed{}$ $14 - 9 = \boxed{}$

____ ____ ____ ____

$18 - 2 = \boxed{}$ $7 - 4 = \boxed{}$ $20 - 10 = \boxed{}$ $12 - 7 = \boxed{}$

____ ____

$17 - 2 = \boxed{}$ $20 - 0 = \boxed{}$

____

____ ____ ____ ____ ____ ____.

$16 - 6 = \boxed{}$ $19 - 3 = \boxed{}$ $16 - 15 = \boxed{}$ $19 - 7 = \boxed{}$ $20 - 5 = \boxed{}$ $15 - 12 = \boxed{}$

CODE BOX				
0 = T	3 = L	6 = H	12 = R	16 = P
1 = E	5 = Y	10 = A	15 = I	20 = N

Sand Sounds

Short *a* makes the *ah* sound, as in *cat*.

How many sandcastles do you see?

Sand has the short **a** sound. Find at least **3** other things whose names have the short **a** sound. Circle them and say their names.

What silly things do you see?

Phonics and Spelling: Short a

Hey, Long A!

The long *a* sound can be spelled as *a*-consonant-silent *e*, as in *race*; *ai*, as in *rain*; *ay*, as in *pay*; or *a* alone, as in *April*.

Sort the words in the word bank. Write each word under the picture whose name has the same spelling for the long **a** sound. Say each word as you write it.

baby	braid	cave	day
game	gray	radio	sail

Words with a__e

Words with ai

Words with ay

Words with a alone

Campfire Equations

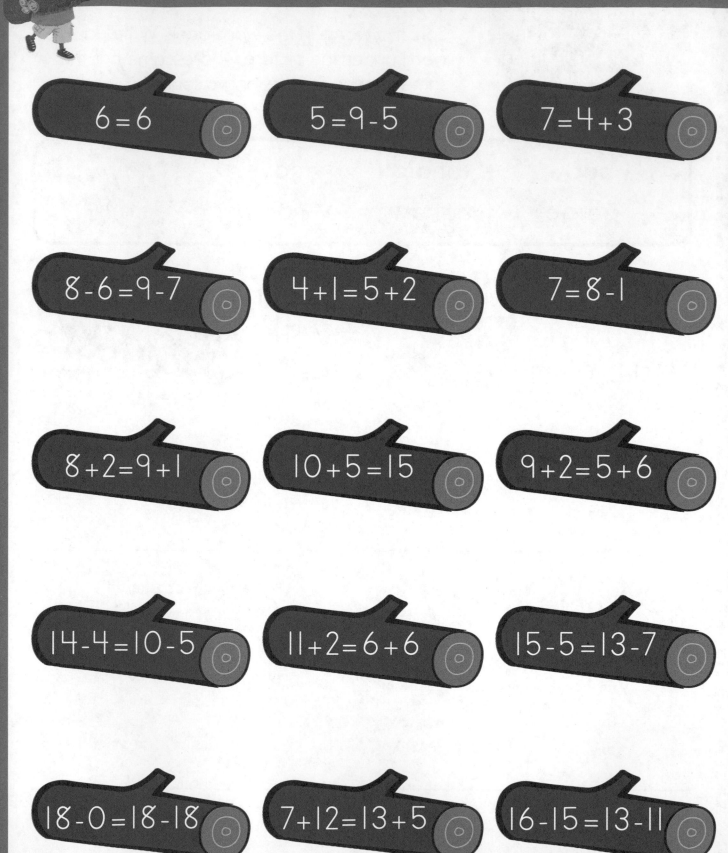

$6 = 6$

$5 = 9 - 5$

$7 = 4 + 3$

$8 - 6 = 9 - 7$

$4 + 1 = 5 + 2$

$7 = 8 - 1$

$8 + 2 = 9 + 1$

$10 + 5 = 15$

$9 + 2 = 5 + 6$

$14 - 4 = 10 - 5$

$11 + 2 = 6 + 6$

$15 - 5 = 13 - 7$

$18 - 0 = 18 - 18$

$7 + 12 = 13 + 5$

$16 - 15 = 13 - 11$

Help Freddy Fox collect logs for the campfire. Circle each equation that is true, and cross out those that are false. Now count the circled equations. How many logs did Freddy collect?

$4-1=3$

$5+3=8+0$

$2+5=7+4$

$6+2=4+3$

$3-3=6-6$

$2-0=2$

$9-5=8-7$

$3-2=7-5$

$10+2=5+7$

$19+1=20$

$16-3=19-6$

$19-7=20-8$

$12+5=4+13$

$8+10=17+3$

$20=19-1$

BONUS!
Summer Craft Activity

Colorful Butterflies

YOU WILL NEED:
- Watercolor paper • Scissors
- Watercolors or acrylic paints
- Chenille stick • Ribbon

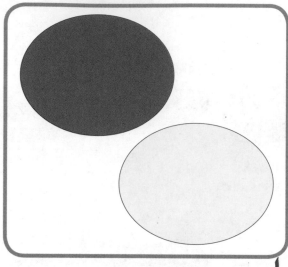

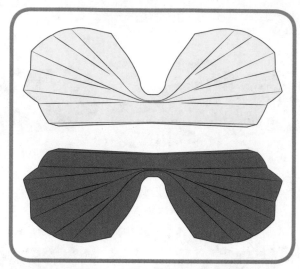

1. With an adult's permission, cut out two oval shapes from watercolor paper.

2. Using watercolors or acrylic paints and water, decorate the ovals. Let them dry.

3. Accordion-fold the ovals. Pinch them together in the middle. Wrap a chenille stick around the center and twist it to form antennae and a body.

4. Add a ribbon hanger.

A group of butterflies is called a *flutter*. Why do you think that is?

Make a flutter to share with friends.

Missing Letters

Write the missing letter in each word using the consonant **n**, **f**, or **d**.

__ork

__eather

__ose

__onkey

lea__

toa__

__oodles

kitte__

__oll

Summer Sparkles

Boom, boom, boom! Fireworks light up the night. What can you tell about the people watching the fireworks?

High-Frequency Words: Question Words; Grammar: Write Questions

Who, *what*, *when*, *where*, *why*, and *how* are question words. You use them to ask questions about something or someone. Use a question word to complete each question below.

_____ many people are watching the fireworks?

_____ is sitting on a blanket?

_____ is an owl sitting?

_____ are some fireworks red, white, and blue?

· ·

Use each question word below to write another question about the picture.

When

_____

_____

What

_____

_____

Where

_____

_____

Make a Ten!

Use the **make-a-10 strategy** to add more easily. Here's how.

9 + 8 = ?

First show 9. Then show 8.

Make a 10. Fill up the 10-frame.

Then add the 7 remaining yellow circles to 10.

10 + 7 = 17

So, 9 + 8 = 17

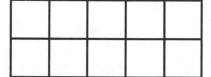

· ·

Your turn! The red circles are already drawn for you. Draw in the yellow circles to make a **10** and find the sum.

9 + 4 =

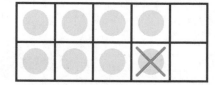

· ·

6 + 5 =

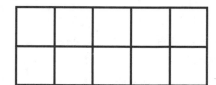

· ·

8 + 7 =

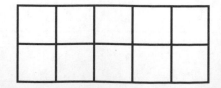

Operations: Addition 0 to 20

Sunshine Stumper

Use the **make-a-10 strategy** to solve each addition problem. Then look at the code box. On the line, write the letter that matches the sum of each problem. The code box will help you solve the riddle. We did the first one to get you started.

Why did the sun go to school?

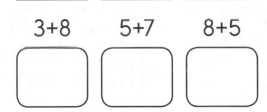

T	
4+9	7+7
13	

3+8	5+7	8+5

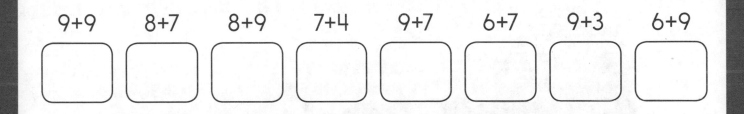

9+9	8+7	8+9	7+4	9+7	6+7	9+3	6+9

CODE BOX
11 = G   12 = E   13 = T   14 = O   15 = R
16 = H   17 = I   18 = B   19 = A

Top Pup!

What do dogs like to eat in a movie theater? *Pup-corn!*

Write the letter **t** or **p** to complete the words in the story.

Spot and I are at the ___et sho___.
She ___aps me with her ___aw. I
know what she wants. "Yes, you may
get a ___oy," I say. Will she ___ick
a ___an cat or a red boo___? No.
Spo___ runs by the ___oys. She
found something better: her friend,
a ___uppy named Do___!

Sticker Collection

Natalie collects groups of stickers. You can show the number in each group as a ten and extra ones. For example:

 19 stars = 1 ten and 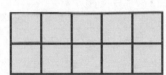 9 ones

Complete each problem. Color in the 10-frame to show **10**.
Then draw the extra ones in the box provided.

 15 hearts = 1 ten and 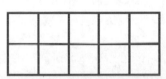 ones

 17 smiley = 1 ten and 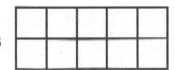 ones
faces

 12 suns = 1 ten and  ones

Yak with a Kayak

Help this yak reach the river so she can launch her kayak! Write **< (less than)**, **> (greater than)**, or **= (equal to)** to complete each statement. Then follow the **greater than** symbols to move from start to finish.

The arrow of each symbol always points to the smaller number.

START

42 ☐ 25

56 ☐ 54

73 ☐ 84

21 ☐ 26

93 ☐ 39

FINISH

77 ☐ 57

23 ☐ 23

98 ☐ 98

28 ☐ 19

16 ☐ 16

Challenge:
Last month, 548 boaters rode on the river. The month before, 427 rode on it.

548 ☐ 427

Just Asking

Sadie has a mystery to solve. Write 6 questions that will help her crack the case. Begin with the words below. Put a question mark at the end of each sentence. We did one to get you started.

What _What happened to the flowerpot?_

How _____

_____

Did _____

_____

When _____

_____

Who _____

_____

Will _____

_____

What's Missing?

7 + 3 = ☐   ☐ + 3 = 13

6 + 6 = ☐   ☐ + 5 = 17

8 + ☐ = 11   15 = 9 + ☐

7 + ☐ = 16   20 = 10 + ☐

☐ + 5 = 9   19 + ☐ = 19

Circle the differences you see between these pictures.

Write the missing number that makes each equation true.

14 − 0 = ☐   ☐ − 9 = 9

18 − 9 = ☐   ☐ − 3 = 17

12 − ☐ = 10   5 = ☐ − 3

15 − ☐ = 5   0 = ☐ − 20

☐ − 7 = 11   15 = ☐ − 4

Write with E's

Write the letter **e** to complete these short-vowel words. Say each word aloud.

h__n

l__mon

j__t

sh__ll

n__st

st__m

10

t__n

sl__d

Sleepy Sheep

Read each long-**e** word in the word bank. The words are scrambled in the poem below. Unscramble and write each word to complete the poem.

field   green   heap   leaping   peep
please   sheep   sleeping   speak   squeak

Shh! Do not (kesap) _____!

Mice, do not (qsakeu) _____!

The (hepse) _____ are napping

on hay in a (aphe) _____.

In a (delif) _____ of

(eergn) _____ grass,

they spent the day (ginaple) _____.

So now it is time

for them to be (pselgnie) _____.

So don't make a sound.

Not even a (epep) _____!

Be very quiet

and let them nap, (aeslep) _____!

Check the Time

Read the time on each clock. Write that time in the digital clock on the right. We did the first one to get you started.

 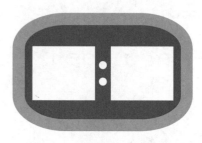

 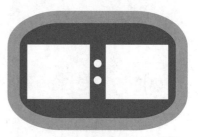

Read the time on each digital clock. Draw hands on the clock on the right to show the same time. We did the first one to get you started.

The little hand points to the hour. The big hand points to the minute.

 2:00

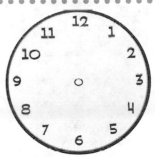

 8:30

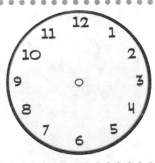

 3:00

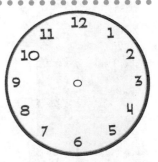

 1:30

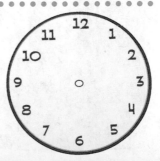

 5:00

Block Towers

Read each number. Rewrite the number as a number of tens. Then color in that number of tens blocks. We did the first one for you.

60 = [6] tens

50 = [ ] tens

20 = [ ] tens

80 = [ ] tens

70 = [ ] tens

30 = [ ] tens

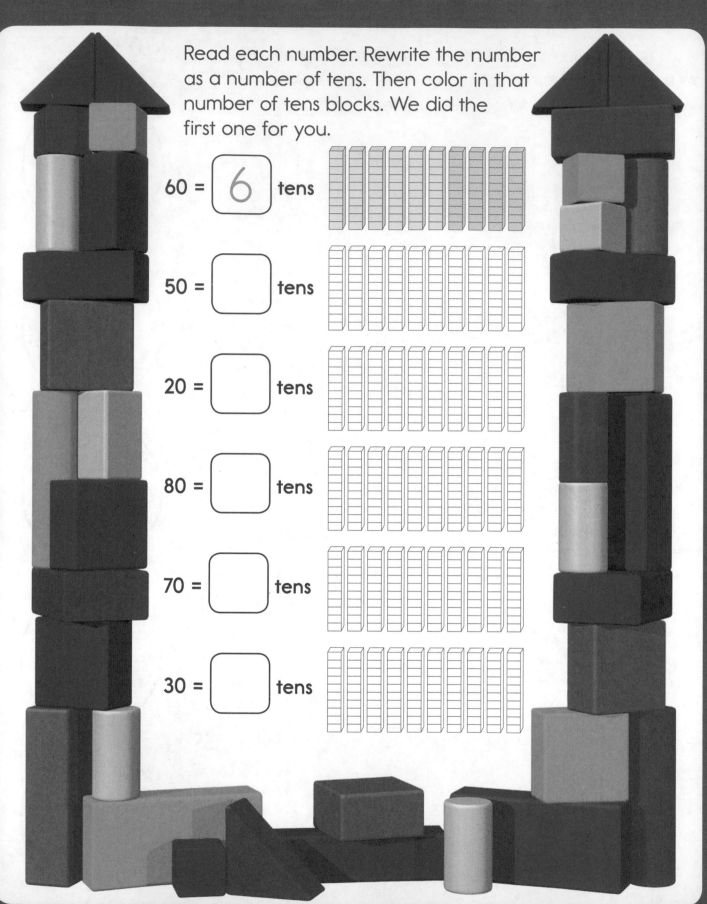

Make a Gift Basket

YOU WILL NEED:
- Cardboard basket
- Tempera paint
- Markers
- Ribbon
- Chenille sticks

1. With an adult's permission, paint the outside of a cardboard basket with tempera paint. Allow the paint to dry overnight.

2. Decorate the basket with markers. Weave ribbon in and out of the holes in the basket.

3. Ask an adult to help tie the ribbon in a bow and make holes near the top of the basket. Use chenille sticks to make one or two handles.

Fill your basket with treats or flowers and surprise someone!

How do you feel when someone gives you a surprise gift?

Beach Day!

Write your own word problem about a day at the beach. Give it to a friend to solve.

It's a beautiful day for the beach. Solve these word problems about the children at the beach.

There are **4** children building a sandcastle. Some more children come to help. Now there are **7** children building the sandcastle. How many children came to help?

$$4 + \boxed{} = 7$$

There are **3** children playing in the water. Then **4** girls and **6** boys join them in the water. How many children are in the water now?

$$3 + 4 + 6 = \boxed{}$$

Arram and Maria are collecting shells. Maria has **16** shells. Arram has **4** fewer shells than Maria. How many shells does Arram have?

$$16 - 4 = \boxed{}$$

There are **11** children eating a snack. **8** of them are eating apples. The rest of the children are eating oranges. How many children are eating oranges?

$$11 - 8 = \boxed{}$$

Find and circle the **9** objects in this Hidden Pictures® puzzle.

harmonica · fried egg · doughnut · postage stamp · fish

canoe · ruler · plum · watermelon

Coastal Colors

banana

umbrella

hot dog

baseball

popcorn

cookie

button

ruler

Tell about the picture. Write a color word to complete each sentence.

| blue | brown | orange |
| pink | purple | red | white | yellow |

Three kids ride in a _____ boat.

One girl has a _____ hat.

They spot an _____ seahorse.

A _____ whale swims by.

The _____ octopus waves "hello."

A _____ sea star is nearby.

The sky has _____ puffy clouds.

Two palm trees grow on the _____ sand.

Time for Dessert

Count the number of dessert items in each group. How many tens and ones are in the group? Circle the ten in each group. Then, draw a line from each group to its matching place-value chart.

○   ○

Tens	Ones
1	3

○   ○

Tens	Ones
1	6

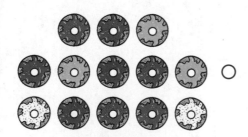

○   ○

Tens	Ones
1	4

○   ○

Tens	Ones
1	1

Missing Letters

Why was the horse sneezing? *Because she had a little colt*

Write the beginning of each word using the consonant **h** or **r**. The clues on the left describe the word.

Not cold   ____ot

A small animal with big ears   ____abbit

All the colors of the _____   ____ainbow

It says *neigh.*   ____orse

This flower smells sweet.   ____ose

You can clap your _____.   ____ands

It is on top of a house.   ____oof

It grows on your head.   ____air

Which Word?

Base words are stand-alone words that have meaning all by themselves.

Circle the word that best completes each sentence.

I ride the (away/subway) to the bookstore.

I buy a book about (friendship/friendly).

Another book I want is not out yet, so I will (preorder/reorder) it.

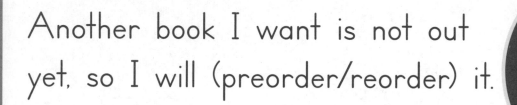

A prefix is added to the beginning of a base word. A suffix is added to the end of a base word. Prefixes and suffixes change the base word's meaning.

The store's plush cushions are so (comfortable/comforting).

Be (careful/careless)! That book is heavy.

When I get home, Mom will (reheat/unheat) lunch for me.

Vocabulary: Affixes

The Weirdest Ride

Read the story. Then look at each word in bold type. Underline its base word and circle the ending.

Mom and I went to the mall. We visited four **stores**, and I bought two **dresses**. After a quick stop to refuel the car, we **headed** home. Suddenly, a monkey **appeared**. He jumped onto a fruit truck and started **eating**. Behind the truck was an unusual driver—an alligator. It was the **weirdest** drive home ever!

The endings *s* and *es* can be used to make nouns plural, or more than one. The ending *ed* is used to show that an action happened in the past.

The suffix *er* is used to compare two things. The suffix *est* is used to compare three or more things.

What silly things do you see in the picture?

At the Candy Store

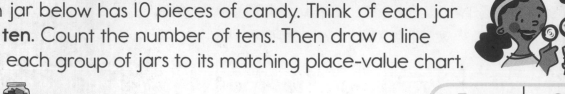

Each jar below has 10 pieces of candy. Think of each jar as a **ten**. Count the number of tens. Then draw a line from each group of jars to its matching place-value chart.

 ○   ○

Tens	Ones
2	0

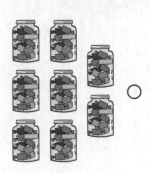 ○   ○

Tens	Ones
8	0

 ○   ○

Tens	Ones
5	0

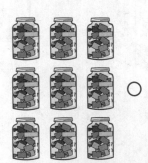 ○   ○

Tens	Ones
4	0

○   ○

Tens	Ones
9	0

Enjoy Your Lunch!

Look at the picture. Think of a word to complete each command. Write it on the line. Then add a period or exclamation mark.

A command is a sentence that tells someone to do something. A command ends with a period or an exclamation point.

Please _____ my hand

Say _____ when you order your food

Look out for the _____

Please take this _____

....

Write 3 exclamations that a person might say about food. We did one to get you started.

This is delicious!

_____

_____

An exclamation is a sentence that shows a strong feeling or a sound. An exclamation ends with an exclamation point.

Climb to the Top

The mice on the next page are climbing to the top of the wall. Who will get there first? For each row of equations, circle the true equation under A, B, or C. Then shade a square in the matching column. As you do, the mice climb to the top. Which mouse will win?

A	B	C
$5+8 = 11+4$	$3+9 = 9+3$	$0+4 = 4+10$
$9+8 = 17+3$	$3+7 = 5+6$	$11+6 = 14+3$
$4+1 = 2+2$	$3+5 = 7+1$	$6+13 = 7+6$
$14+5 = 15+4$	$11+9 = 18+1$	$7+9 = 14+3$
$9+7 = 13+3$	$3+3 = 5+0$	$10+6 = 13+4$
$8+8 = 9+7$	$10+2 = 3+11$	$5+4 = 7+1$
$13+2 = 7+7$	$3+6 = 4+7$	$14+0 = 8+6$
$6-2 = 8-6$	$17-2 = 20-6$	$19-3 = 20-4$
$15-2 = 14-1$	$16-14 = 5-2$	$14-3 = 18-8$
$13-11 = 19-18$	$20-2 = 18-0$	$12-2 = 2-2$

Operations: Addition and Subtraction 0 to 20

A	B	C
20–4 = 16–6	15–9 = 17–6	20–5 = 17–2
16–3 = 19–5	14–7 = 19–13	10–0 = 18–8
15–5 = 11–2	9–2 = 17–10	10–9 = 18–6
14–9 = 15–6	18–2 = 15–3	16–8 = 18–10

A	B	C

Silly Dreams

Read this silly story. Find and circle at least **15** words with the short *i* sound. Say each word as you circle it.

Hi! I'm Tim. Last night I had a funny dream. In the dream, there was a pig with wings. It zipped across the sky and landed on a pink barn.

The pig looked down and saw a cow with a wig. Then a fish bounced by on a pogo stick! Then in a flash, the fish changed into a pickle. How silly!

It's I Time

Fill in this grid with the long-*i* words listed below. Use the number of letters in each word as a clue to where it might fit. We did one to get you started.

The long *i* sound can be spelled as *i*-consonant-silent *e*, as in *slice*; *igh*, as in *fright*; *ie*, as in *lie*; or *i* alone, as in *iron*.

3 Letters
PIE
TIE

4 Letters
KITE
MICE
MIND
~~SIGH~~
TIDE
VINE
WILD

5 Letters
DRIVE
GLIDE
NIGHT
SHINE
SMILE

6 Letters
BRIGHT
STRIPE

S I G H

A Dino and Digits

Count on to add. Use the number line. Start with the greater number. We did the first one for you.

10 + 3 = [13] E

40 + 2 = [ ] I

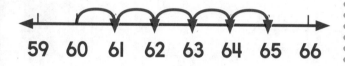

60 + 5 = [ ] G

80 + 4 = [ ] H

2 + 30 = [ ] T

90 + 6 = [ ] A

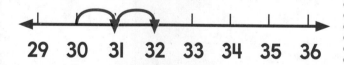

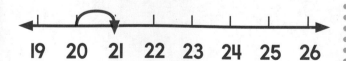

1 + 20 = [ ] T

5 + 50 = [ ] E

Use the letters next to your answers to solve the riddle below.

What was *T. rex*'s favorite number?

___ ___ ___ ___ ___ (___ ___ ___)
55 42 65 84 21   96 32 13

BONUS!
Summer Craft Activity

Make a Sailboat

YOU WILL NEED:
- Paper • Scissors
- Crayons or markers • Glue • Plastic straw
- Clay • Clean foam tray

1. With an adult's permission, cut a paper sail. Draw on one side of your sail. Fold the sail in half. Make sure your drawing is on the outside.

2. Open the sail. Put glue on the side with no drawings.

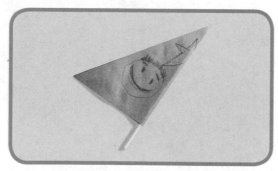

3. Put the straw in the middle and fold the sail. Let the glue dry.

4. Use clay to attach the sail to the tray.

Make sails of different sizes. Does the sail size affect how your boat moves?

Missing Letters

Write the missing letter in each word using the consonant **b** or **c**.

__elery

__anana

The letter c makes a soft sound (s) when it is in front of the letters i, y, or e. You can hear soft c in the word city.

__anjo

__ulb

__ent

__ircle

bi__

__ircus

Busy Day

Nick has a full schedule today. Each clock below shows the time of an event in his day. Read the time on each clock. Then write the name of the event in the schedule under the matching time.

8:00 AM

_____

8:30 AM

_____

9:00 AM

_____

11:00 AM

_____

1:00 PM

_____

2:00 PM

_____

5:30 PM

_____

walk dog

lunch

wake up

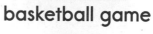

basketball game

piano lesson

breakfast

dinner

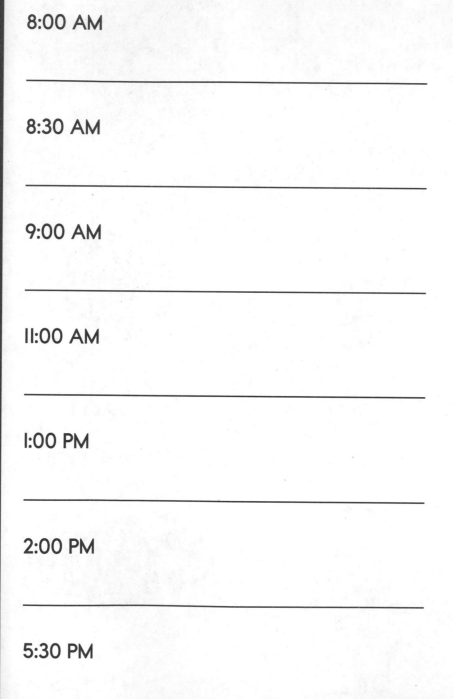

Time Out!

It's time for a riddle! Read the time on each clock. Then write each clock's letter in the space above the matching digital time.

What do workers do in a clock factory?

___ ___ ___ ___   ___ ___ ___ ___ ___
6:00 1:30 3:00 10:30   8:00 1:30 11:30 10:30 9:00

At Camp Yippee

Camp Yippee is lots of fun! What silly things do you see in the picture?

High-Frequency Words: Prepositions

Tell about what is happening at the camp. Complete each sentence with a preposition from the word bank. Use each word only once.

| across | along | at | in | on | with |

1. There are many people _____ Camp Yippee.

2. Some people are swimming _____ the lake.

3. A lifeguard is sitting _____ a white chair.

4. Three men walk _____ a path.

5. In the yellow canoe, three people ride _____ a penguin.

6. _____ from the yellow canoe, other people ride with a raccoon.

Sandy's Strategy

Sandy's favorite number is 10. Why? Finding 10 makes subtraction easier. Sandy uses a subtraction strategy called **decomposing**, or breaking apart, numbers to use a 10 to subtract.

STEP 1:
I know that **13 – 3** will be **10**.
So I break apart **4** into **3** and **1**.

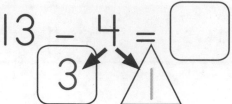

$$13 - 4 = \boxed{}$$
$$\boxed{3} \quad \triangle{1}$$

STEP 2:
Next I subtract **3** from **13** to find **10**.

$$13 - \boxed{3} = 10$$

STEP 3:
Then I subtract **1** from **10** to get **9**.

$$10 - \triangle{1} = \boxed{9}$$

SO . . .
The difference between **13** and **4** is **9**.

$$13 - 4 = \boxed{9}$$

Use Sandy's strategy to solve these subtraction problems.

$$14 - 6 = \boxed{}$$
$$\boxed{} \quad \triangle$$

$$14 - \boxed{} = 10$$

$$10 - \triangle = \boxed{}$$

SO . . .
$$14 - 6 = \boxed{}$$

$$16 - 7 = \boxed{}$$
$$\boxed{} \quad \triangle$$

$$16 - \boxed{} = 10$$

$$10 - \triangle = \boxed{}$$

SO . . .
$$16 - 7 = \boxed{}$$

Sandy needs help finding her way back to her beach towel. Write the missing number to complete each problem. Then, follow the numbers you wrote **in order from 2 to 9** to help Sandy find the correct path.

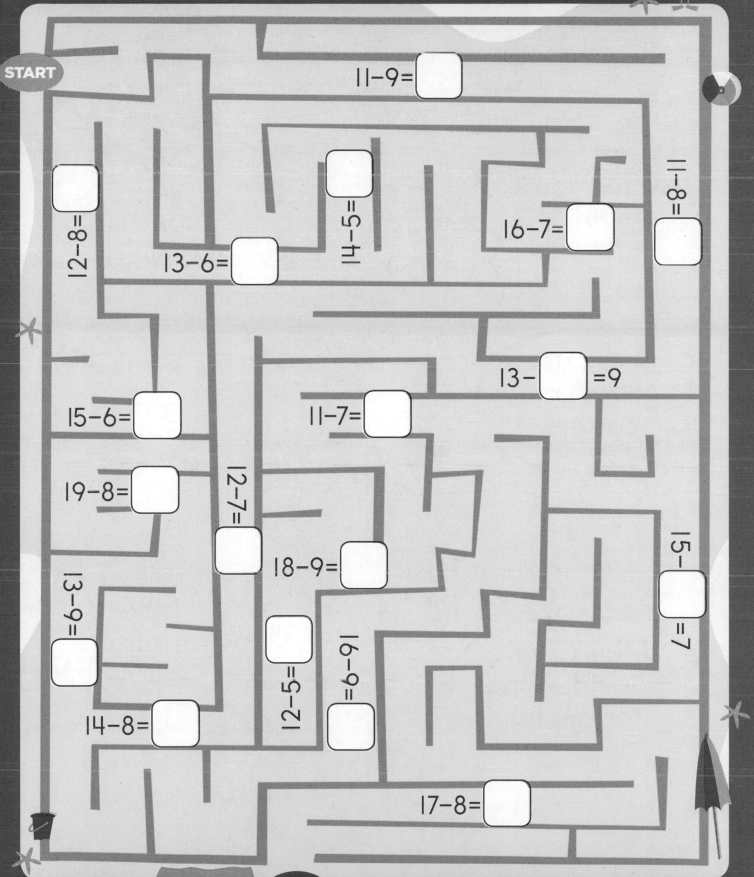

START

$11-9=$ ☐

$11-5=$ ☐

$16-7=$ ☐

$11-8=$ ☐

$12-8=$ ☐

$13-6=$ ☐

$13-$ ☐ $=9$

$15-6=$ ☐

$11-7=$ ☐

$19-8=$ ☐

$12-7=$ ☐

$18-9=$ ☐

$15-$ ☐ $=7$

$13-9=$ ☐

$16-9=$ ☐

$12-5=$ ☐

$14-8=$ ☐

$17-8=$ ☐

FINISH

What's That?

Each cat at the party has something to say—but is it a statement, a command, a question, or an exclamation? Put a period, a question mark, or an exclamation point at the end of each sentence. We did the first one to get you started.

> There are 4 kinds of sentences: statements, commands, questions, **and** exclamations.

Would you like to dance?

Oh, yes I would

These are oatmeal cookies

Eat another

May I have a turn

I think I am done dunking for apples

Kangaroo Clean-Up

Write the letter **k** or **l** to complete the words in the poem.

"What will I do?" asked the ___angaroo.

"There's no room for my joey in my pocket."

She emptied it out and found a ___azoo,

a ___ettle, a ___amp, and a ___ocket.

Then she found a ___izard and a ___adder,

her ___eys, a ___iwi and a ___ite.

Now the pocket has plenty of room,

and her joey can fit just right!

Coaster Maze

START

$18 - 7 =$

$2 + 10 =$

$6 - 5 =$

$-2 = 15$

$-4 = 0$

$1 +$

$-4 = 6$

$17 -$

$16 -$

$= 3$

$= 11$

$+ 5 = 8$

$= 10$

$-10 = 10$

$9 + 5 =$

$+ 1 = 5$

$+ 3 = 9$

$0 + 7 =$

$= 19$

$16 -$

$= 5$

$8 +$

$18 - 9 =$

$-13 = 3$

$9 =$

$+ 4 = 17$

$17 = 19 -$

$+ 0$

1 $+ 0 = 1$

Find a path for this roller-coaster car. First, solve these problems. Write the missing numbers to make the equations true. Then follow the numbers you wrote in counting order from 1 to 20 to the finish.

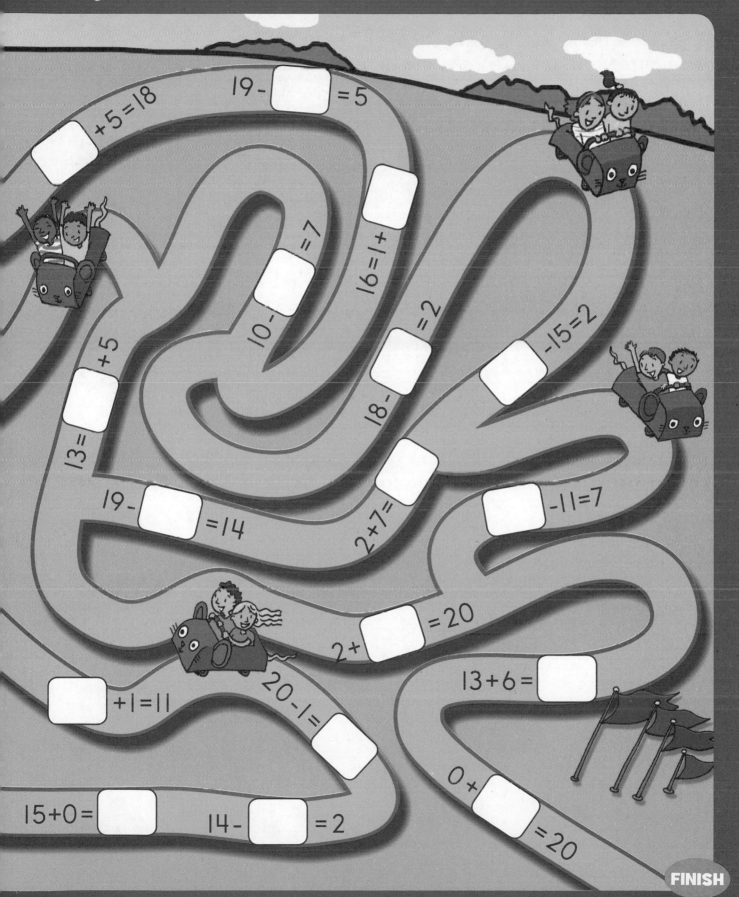

$+5 = 18$

$19 - \boxed{} = 5$

$16 = 1 + \boxed{}$

$10 - \boxed{} = 7$

$\boxed{} - 15 = 2$

$18 - \boxed{} = 2$

$13 = \boxed{} + 5$

$2 + 7 = \boxed{}$

$\boxed{} - 11 = 7$

$19 - \boxed{} = 14$

$2 + \boxed{} = 20$

$13 + 6 = \boxed{}$

$\boxed{} + 1 = 11$

$20 - 1 = \boxed{}$

$15 + 0 = \boxed{}$

$14 - \boxed{} = 2$

$0 + \boxed{} = 20$

FINISH

65

You've Got This!

Write the letter **o** to complete each short-**o** word. Then draw a line from each word to the picture it matches.

l___g ○ ○

s___ck ○ ○

d___ll ○ ○

f___x ○ ○

r___ck ○ ○

m___p ○ ○

d___lphin ○ ○

Go, Gopher!

Help Grover Gopher get back home. Follow only words with the long **o** sound from START to FINISH.

The long *o* sound can be spelled as *o–consonant–silent e*, as in *note*; *oa*, as in *moat*; *oe*, as in *Joe*; *ow*, as in *low*; or *o* alone, as in *piano*.

START

road
no
pot
cop
goal
slot
grow
flop
foam
fog
doe
zone
dog
toast
boat
robe
rope
nose
joke

FINISH

Peacock and Crow

Read the folktale. Then answer the questions on the next page.

A Folktale from Thailand

Long ago, all birds had white feathers. One day Peacock got tired of his plain feathers. "Will you paint my feathers?" Peacock asked Crow.

"Gladly," said Crow. "And then you can paint mine."

Crow painted and painted. He became hungry. But Peacock wanted more colors. Crow kept painting. His stomach growled. But now Peacock wanted spots.

At last, Peacock was happy. He strutted to show off his fancy feathers.

"Now I will paint you," he told Crow.

Crow grabbed a pot of black paint. "Just use this and please hurry. I am so hungry!"

Peacock quickly splashed black paint on Crow, and Crow flew off to find food.

To this day, all crows have black feathers, and all peacocks have colorful feathers. Peacock still likes to show off, and Crow is always looking for another meal.

1. Who asks Crow to paint his feathers? Why?

_____

_____

2. What does it mean that crow's "stomach growled"?

_____

_____

3. What happens when it is Peacock's turn to paint Crow?

_____

_____

4. What does this folktale explain about peacocks and crows?

_____

_____

_____

Missing Letters

Write the missing letter in each word using the consonant **g**, **q**, or **w**.

__ueen

__oat

__agon

do__

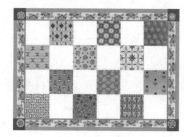

__uilt

__ater

fla__

win__

__lasses

BONUS!
Summer Fun Recipe

Red, White, and Blue Nachos

YOU WILL NEED:
- 6-ounce bag blue tortilla chips
- 1 cup salsa
- 1 cup shredded white cheddar cheese
- Optional toppings: chopped tomatoes, sliced olives, black beans rinsed and drained

Before You Begin
Ask an adult to set the oven to broil.

Do you think these nachos would be a good snack for the Fourth of July? Why or why not?

1. Spread tortilla chips evenly on the bottom of a 9-inch-by-13-inch pan.

2. Spoon the salsa over the chips.

3. Sprinkle the cheese on top. Add toppings, if you'd like. Ask an adult to broil for 3 minutes. Let it cool for 3 minutes before eating.

Walk, Jog, Run

It's a busy day in the park! Many people are moving about—but they don't all move in the same way. Circle the strongest verb that best completes each sentence.

1. A girl (moves/passes/zooms) by on a skateboard.

2. Another girl walks a poodle. The dog (struts/walks/crawls) with its head held high.

3. Heads up! Here comes a disc (flipping/flying/falling) toward us.

4. The angry man (strolls/chases/creeps) after the squirrel.

5. A soccer ball (hits/springs/bounces) off that girl's foot.

6. There's a statue at the edge of the park. A boy (snaps/takes/considers) a picture of it.

Different verbs can describe similar actions. Some of the verbs may be stronger than others. You can use these *shades of meaning* to pick just the right verb in your writing.

Do You Mean?

Draw a line to match each pair of adjectives with a third adjective that has a similar meaning, but is more intense or stronger.

warm, hot ○   ○ filthy

amusing, funny ○   ○ overjoyed

dusty, messy ○   ○ fluffy

tired, weary ○   ○ gigantic

big, huge ○   ○ booming

mad, angry ○   ○ silent

glad, happy ○   ○ hilarious

quiet, hushed ○   ○ exhausted

soft, fuzzy ○   ○ furious

loud, noisy ○   ○ sizzling

What goes from damp to wet to soaking the more it dries?

A towel!

Fruit Families

Using fact families can make addition and subtraction easier. Fill in the boxes to complete the addition and subtraction families.

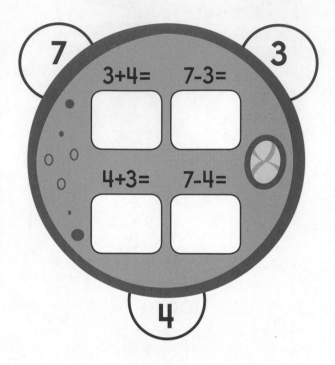

7 · 3 · 4

3+4=

7-3=

4+3=

7-4=

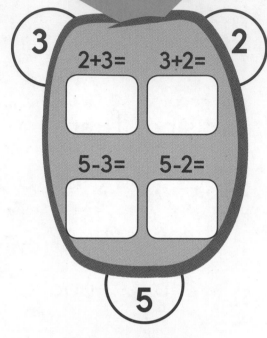

3 · 2 · 5

2+3=

3+2=

5-3=

5-2=

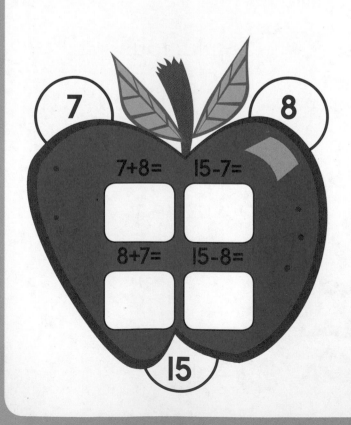

7 · 8 · 15

7+8=

15-7=

8+7=

15-8=

5 · 6 · 11

5+6=

11-6=

11-5=

6+5=

9 9+8= **8**

17-8=

8+9= 17-9=

17

7 6+7= 13-7= **6**

13-6= 7+6=

13

7 7+9= 16-9= **9**

9+7= 16-7=

16

8 8+4= 12-8= **4**

12-4= 4+8=

12

Missing Letters

Write the missing letter in each word using the consonant **j** or **x**. The clues on the left describe the word.

This flies very fast.   ___et

An animal that rhymes with "rocks"   fo___

A big cat with spots   ___aguar

It is often made of cardboard.   bo___

Peanut butter and _____   ___elly

This shows bones.   ___-ray

A glass of orange _____   ___uice

Missing Letters

The letter *g* can make a soft sound (*j*) when it is in front of the letters *i*, *y*, or *e*. You can hear soft *g* in the word *gym*.

Write the beginning of each word using the consonant **g** or **v**.

_ulture

_et

_iolin

_ase

_iraffe

_iant

_olcano

_ems

_an

Count and Graph

78   Data: Organize, Represent, and Interpret Data

Draw the objects you counted to complete the picture graph. We did the first row to get you started.

How Many Things?

Toothbrushes				
Soccer Balls				
Keys				

Use the graph to answer the questions.

1. How many keys are there? _____

2. Are there fewer toothbrushes or keys? _____

3. How many more balls are there than toothbrushes? _____

4. How many objects does the graph show in all? _____

79

Go, Team, Go!

Can you find the 10 objects in this Hidden Pictures® puzzle?

arrow • slice of watermelon • ring • spoon • funnel • ruler • fish • ladder • magnet • needle

Describe the picture of the basketball game. Write a preposition from the word bank to complete each sentence. Use each word only once.

Some prepositions, such as *above*, *below*, and *next to*, describe position.

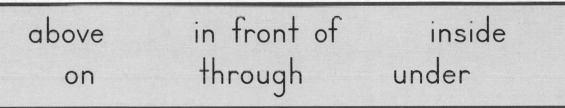

above	in front of	inside
on	through	under

1. There's a basketball game _____ the gym.

2. A band plays _____ the basketball court.

3. The players look to see if the ball will go _____ the hoop.

4. A player on the purple team waits _____ the hoop to get the ball.

5. Fans sit _____ the bleachers.

6. Banners hang on the wall _____ their heads.

Shape Search

Say each shape name in the word bank. Point to the correct shape as you say the name. Then find each of the **7** shapes in the picture below.

circle	heart	oval	rectangle
square	star	triangle	

Geometry: Attributes of Shapes

Draw Shapes

Use crayons or markers to color in the shapes you draw.

Draw each shape named below. Then fill in the blank in each sentence.

Square

Triangle

A square has ☐ sides.

A triangle has ☐ sides.

Circle

Rectangle

A circle has ☐ corners.

A rectangle has ☐ long sides that are equal length and ☐ short sides that are equal length.

Pup's Mud Run

Help Pup jump in all the mud puddles on the way to his food bowl! Write the letter **u** in each short-**u** word. Say each word as you write it.

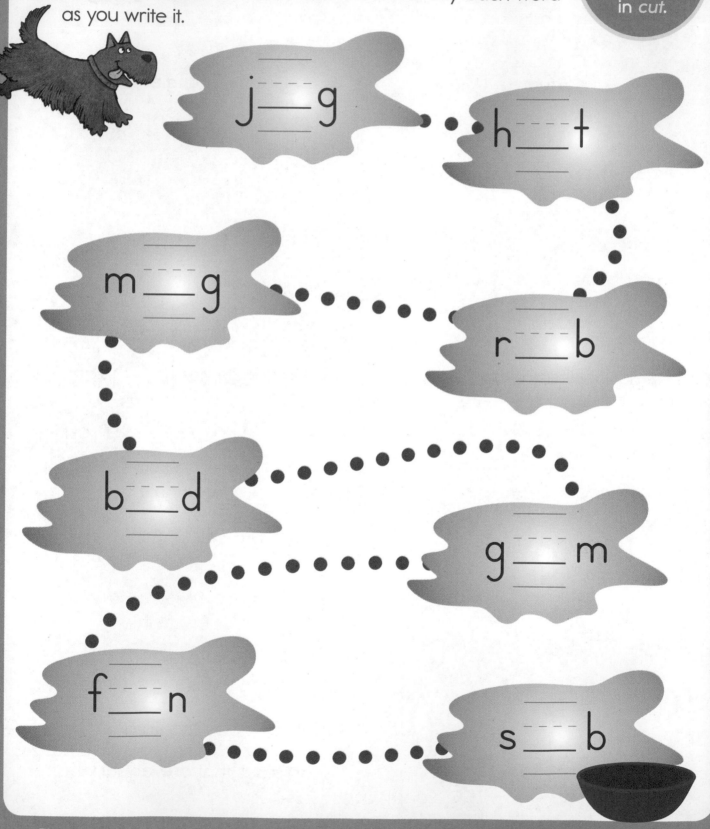

j__g

h__t

m__g

r__b

b__d

g__m

f__n

s__b

Just for U

There are **20** words that have the long **u** sound hidden in this grid. Look for them up, down, across, and diagonally. After you've circled them all, write the leftover letters in order from left to right and top to bottom. They will spell out the answer to the riddle. We've circled one word to get you started.

AMUSE
BLUE
CLUE
CUBE
CUTE
DUE
FEW
FLU
FUME
GLUE
HUGE
HUMAN
LUTE
MULE
MUSIC
NEW
PLUME
UNICORN
UNIFORM
USEFUL

C	U	B	E	E	Y	G	L	U	E
O	U	G	S	C	A	U	N	N	T
U	U	U	N	E	A	S	W	I	P
H	M	U	S	I	C	E	I	C	A
A	F	N	O	B	F	F	U	O	F
P	L	U	M	E	T	U	E	R	U
C	U	Y	L	O	U	L	U	N	M
H	U	B	C	U	A	N	L	N	E
U	O	T	L	T	T	T	C	D	U
M	N	E	E	U	A	E	F	U	N
A	M	U	L	E	E	I	S	E	E
N	H	U	N	I	F	O	R	M	W

What is the difference between a piano and a fish?

— — — — — — — —

— — — — — — — ,

— — — — — — — —

— — — — — — — — !

Dance the Blues Away

Read the poem. Then answer the questions.

Feeling grumpy?
Got the blues?
Slip into your
    dancing shoes.
There's nothing that
    will banish
        gloom like
tapping through
the dining room.

1. Which word from the poem is another word for *dancing*?

   ○ shoes   ○ tapping   ○ dining

2. Which pair of words helps create rhythm in the poem?

   ○ grumpy/blues   ○ banish/gloom   ○ blues/shoes

3. Write a word from the poem that rhymes with *gloom*. _____

4. How does the author most likely feel about dancing? Why do you think so?

   _____

   _____

5. Does the poem make you feel sad or happy? Which words in the poem help you feel this way?

   _____

   _____

Track the Moon

BONUS!
Summer Science Activity

Why do you think the moon looks different at different times of the month?

1. When you go outside, look up to the sky. During the day, you may see clouds, the sun, and the moon. At night, you may see stars and the moon. Each time you see the moon, it may be in a different part of the sky. When the moon looks like a round circle, it is called a full moon. What does the moon look like in the night sky? Does it look the same in the day?

2. With an adult's permission, go outside tonight to look at the moon. Draw a picture of what it looks like. You can also write what you notice about the moon. Repeat this for a few days, then look back at your drawings. What do you notice about the moon?

From Y to Z!

There are **19** words that start with **y** or **z** hidden in this grid. Look for them up, down, across, and diagonally. After you've circled them all, write the leftover letters in order from left to right and top to bottom. They will spell out the answer to the riddle. We've circled the first word to get you started.

~~YAK~~
YAM
YARD
YARN
YAWN
YEAR
YELL
YES
YET
YOLK
YOU
ZAP
ZEBRA
ZERO
ZIGZAG
ZINNIA
ZIPPER
ZITHER
ZOOM

Y	S	Y	M	I	Z	L	E	S	T
Z	A	Z	E	R	O	H	E	R	E
S	I	W	A	T	O	M	I	L	E
B	E	G	N	T	M	W	E	Y	E
Z	Z	N	Z	Y	A	R	D	A	T
H	I	I	Z	A	E	Y	F	M	P
Y	I	P	T	I	G	A	R	A	Y
E	S	T	P	H	N	R	Z	A	O
S	Y	O	U	E	E	N	N	Y	L
Y	D	L	A	S	R	R	I	E	K
T	A	L	E	Y	E	L	L	A	T
T	E	K	Z	E	B	R	A	R	R

What is the longest word in the dictionary?

_ _ _ _ _ _. _ _ _ _ _

_ _ _ _ _ _ _ _

_ _ _ _ _ _ _ _ _ _

_ _ _ _ _ _ _ _ _ !

At the Carnival

Yuri and his friends are at the carnival. Solve these word problems about what they see and do.

There are 16 cans at the ball-toss booth. 9 cans are red. The rest are blue. How many cans are blue?

$$9 + \boxed{} = 16$$

Yuri had 20 dollars. He spent some money to play a game. Now he has 18 dollars. How many dollars did Yuri spend?

$$\$20 - \$\boxed{} = \$18$$

Yuri used 5 tickets to ride the Ferris wheel, 6 tickets to ride the roller coaster, and 4 tickets to ride the carousel. How many tickets did Yuri use in all?

$$5 + 6 + 4 = \boxed{}$$

Some penguins are riding the Ferris wheel. Then 8 penguins get off. Only 6 penguins are left on the ride. How many penguins were on the Ferris wheel at first?

$$\boxed{} - 8 = 6$$

After going on these rides, Yuri has 3 sheets of 10 tickets each and 5 extra tickets. How many tickets does he have?

$$\boxed{}$$

Find and circle **7** objects in this Hidden Pictures® puzzle.

frying pan

needle

mushroom

envelope

boomerang

wizard's hat

book

The Sea Horse

Read the text about sea horses. When you are finished, answer the questions.

A sea horse is a very unusual fish. Its head looks like a horse's head. It holds onto things with its tail, like a monkey. And, like a mother kangaroo, a sea horse carries its unborn babies in a pouch. But unlike kangaroos, it's the father sea horse that carries the babies in his pouch.

A Male Sea Horse

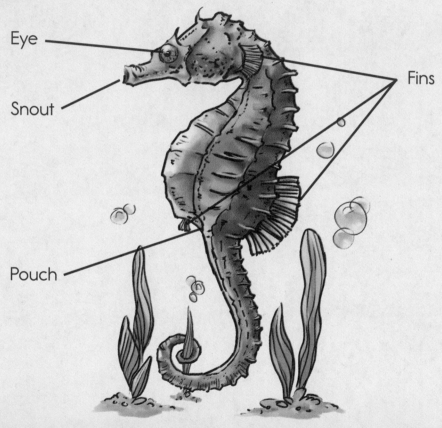

Eye

Snout

Fins

Pouch

What's This?

A dragon? A plant? No! It's a type of sea horse called a leafy sea dragon. When it swims through seaweed, it's hard to spot.

Reading: Informational Text

1. What word parts do you see in the word **unusual**? Use those word parts to help you write a definition of the word.

_____

2. Why are sea horses unusual? Name three reasons the text gives.

_____

_____

_____

3. What does a sea horse use to hold onto things? _____

4. What information does the author give under the heading "What's This?"

_____

_____

5. What does the top picture show? Why do you think the author included it?

_____

_____

Equal Parts

A shape that is divided in half is split into 2 equal parts.

Which shapes are divided in half? Color one half of each shape that is divided in half.

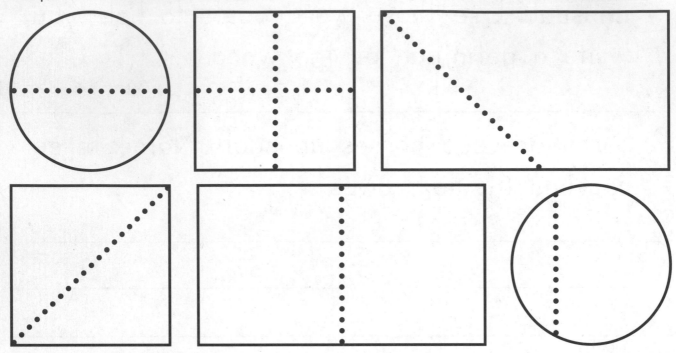

Which shapes are divided into quarters? Color one quarter of each shape that is divided into quarters.

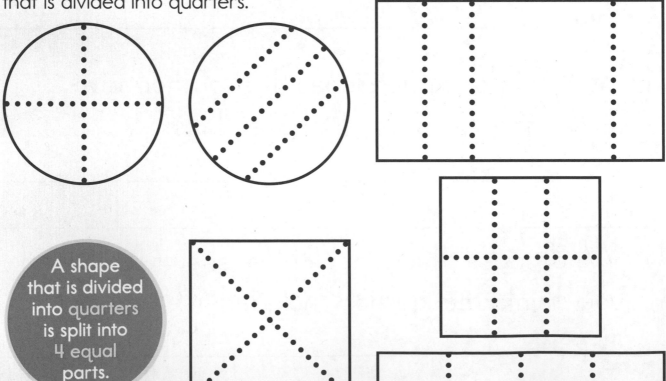

A shape that is divided into quarters is split into 4 equal parts.

Cheese and Crackers

Martin Mouse is collecting food for his family. He wants only crackers and pieces of cheese that are divided into quarters. Follow the crackers and pieces of cheese divided into quarters to help Martin Mouse bring the food back to his home.

whole pieces

Which crackers and pieces of cheese are divided in half?

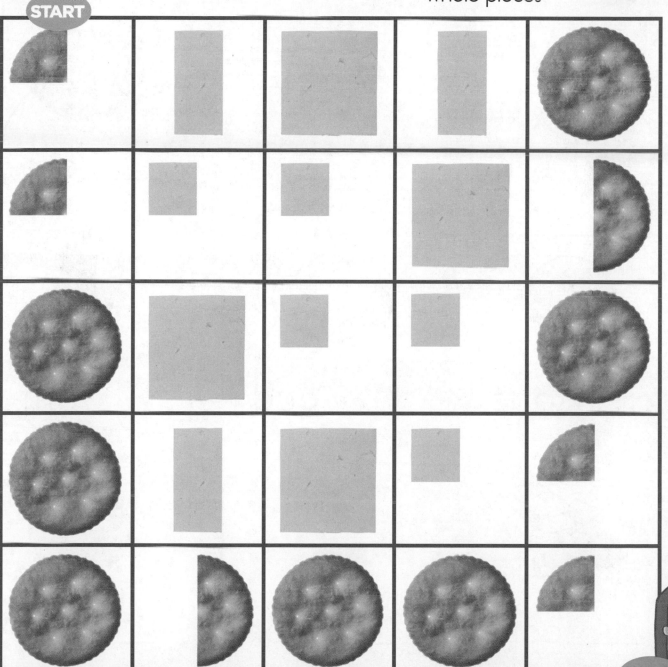

Blend Blanks

Write an *l*-blend to complete each picture name. We did the first one to get you started. You can use a blend more than once.

A *consonant blend* is a group of two or more consonants in which each letter in the group makes its own sound. For example, the *bl* in *black* is a consonant blend.

| bl | cl | fl | gl | pl | sl |

p**l**um   ___y   ___am

___obe   ___oud   ___ant

___ocks   ___ippers   ___ue

Compare Prices

Zeke and his mom are at the store. Help them compare the prices of the items they see. Use **< (less than)**, **> (greater than)**, or **= (equal to)** to complete each statement.

$17 ☐ $24

$19 ☐ $19

$35 ☐ $26

$55 ☐ $58

$12 ☐ $12

$48 ☐ $61

Challenge:
Zeke empties his 2 piggy banks. He has 120 pennies in one and 210 pennies in the other.

120¢ ☐ 210¢

$97 ☐ $89

Time for a Haircut

Circle the shortest comb.

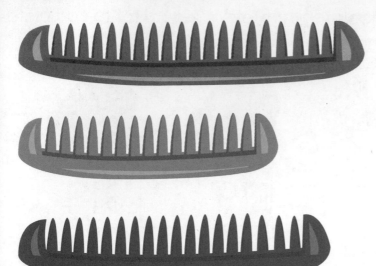

Circle the longest pair of scissors.

Find the hidden fish, leaf, banana, and ladle in this Hidden Pictures® puzzle.

Measurement: Compare Lengths

Tool Shed

Glenda has three sets of tools: hammers, screwdrivers, and saws. Compare the lengths of the tools in each set. Write 1, 2, and 3 to order the tools from shortest to longest.

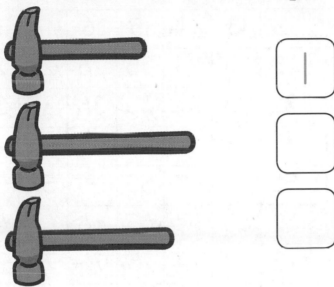

| 1 |

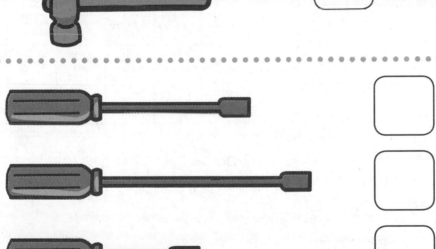

What
kind of
tool does a
prehistoric reptile
carpenter use?

A dino-saw

Calculate This!

You can use a hundred chart to add. Count on by tens.

$$21 + 30 = \boxed{51}$$

1	2	3	4	5	6	7	8	9	10
11	12	13	14	15	16	17	18	19	20
21	22	23	24	25	26	27	28	29	30
31	32	33	34	35	36	37	38	39	40
41	42	43	44	45	46	47	48	49	50
51	52	53	54	55	56	57	58	59	60
61	62	63	64	65	66	67	68	69	70
71	72	73	74	75	76	77	78	79	80
81	82	83	84	85	86	87	88	89	90
91	92	93	94	95	96	97	98	99	100

Start at 21. Count on three tens. 31, 41, 51

Solve each problem on this page and page 101 using the hundred chart. Then use the letters next to the answers to solve the riddle on the next page. We did the first one to get you started.

$$27 + 40 = \boxed{67} \text{ I} \qquad 42 + 40 = \boxed{} \text{ C}$$

$$32 + 10 = \boxed{} \text{ T} \qquad 14 + 50 = \boxed{} \text{ M}$$

$$38 + 20 = \boxed{} \text{ A} \qquad 56 + 30 = \boxed{} \text{ U}$$

$$24 + 30 = \boxed{} \text{ O} \qquad 73 + 20 = \boxed{} \text{ N}$$

$$15 + 20 = \boxed{}\ \text{U}$$
$$18 + 70 = \boxed{}\ \text{N}$$
$$22 + 30 = \boxed{}\ \text{I}$$
$$12 + 80 = \boxed{}\ \text{G}$$

$$33 + 50 = \boxed{}\ \text{O}$$
$$36 + 30 = \boxed{}\ \text{Y}$$
$$24 + 50 = \boxed{}\ \text{O}$$
$$44 + 40 = \boxed{}\ \text{N}$$

What did the student say to the calculator?

I __ __ __ __ __ __ __ __ __ __
67 58 64 82 74 86 84 42 52 88 92

__ __ __ __ __ .
54 93 66 83 35

101

Review It!

A review gives your opinion about something.

Write a review of a place you have visited, such as a playground, a museum, or an amusement park. Tell the name of the place you visited. Explain what you did and did not like not about this place and why. Tell whether you think other people would like the place and explain why.

_____

_____

_____

_____

_____

_____

_____

_____

_____

Draw a picture of your favorite part of the place you visited.

Park the R

The letter *r* makes the vowel that comes before it change to include the *r* sound.

Arrr, mateys! Help Pirate Parker figure out these words! Write **ar** to complete each word. The clues on the left describe each word. Say each word as you write it.

People drive them.   c____s

A kind of container   j____

They shine in the night sky.   st____s

The opposite of small   l____ge

A cat meows, but a dog _____.   b____ks

The opposite of light   d____k

Cows may live on a _____.   f____m

The opposite of soft   h____d

This can cause a fire.   sp____k

You can knit with this.   y____n

Another word for "begin"   st____t

Phonics: R-Controlled A

BONUS!
Summer
Fun
Recipe

Watermelon Pizza

YOU WILL NEED:
- 1 round 1-inch slice of watermelon
- 1 small kiwifruit   • 6 green grapes
- 1 small banana
- 2 tablespoons raspberry or strawberry preserves

Before You Begin
Ask an adult to slice the watermelon and peel the kiwi.

1. Peel and slice the banana. Slice the kiwi and cut the grapes in half.

2. Spread the preserves over the watermelon. Top with the fruit.

3. Ask an adult to cut the watermelon into 6 pieces.

Watermelons are more than 90 percent water! Can you name 3 other very juicy fruits?

Down on the Farm

Doubles facts are easy to remember. That's why you can use them to do addition problems.

> **Here's how:**
> $6 + 7 = ?$
> You know that $6 + 6 = 12$, and 7 is one more than 6.
> So, $6 + 7$ will be one more than 12. $6 + 7 = 13$.

Use doubles to add the numbers below. Then use the letters next to your answers to solve the riddle.

$4 + 5 = \boxed{}$ O $3 + 4 = \boxed{}$ O

$4 + 6 = \boxed{}$ I $5 + 6 = \boxed{}$ C

$7 + 8 = \boxed{}$ S $7 + 6 = \boxed{}$ M

What is a cow's favorite school subject?

___ ___ ___ ___ ___ ___
13   9   7   15   10   11

Only one correct path will lead the farmer to the barn. To find the right path, solve each addition problem using doubles or other strategies. Then follow the numbers you wrote in counting order from **10** to **20** to the finish.

$5+6=$

$6+6=$

$5+5=$

$7+6=$

$6+8=$

$5+4=$

$4+3=$

$3+4=$

$4+6=$

$7+8=$

$8+9=$

$7+9=$

$8+1=$

$9+6=$

$6+3=$

$2+3=$

$8+11=$

$7+2=$

$11+9=$

107

Sprout Some Beans

Read the steps for growing bean plants. When you are finished, answer the questions on the next page.

The roots of plants usually grow underground. If you want to see how they grow, try this!

1. Put some kidney beans in a glass of water. Let the beans soak for 3 hours.

2. Put the beans on a wet paper towel. Fold the paper towel over the beans.

3. Put the paper towel in a zippered plastic bag. Put the bag in a warm, dark place.

4. After 2 or 3 days, roots will appear. Split open one of the beans. You'll see the stem and leaves beginning to grow inside!

5. Now you can grow bean plants. Put the seeds in potting soil with the roots pointing down.

6. Put the plants in a sunny place, and water them regularly.

1. What supplies do you need to sprout bean seeds?

_____

_____

_____

2. What do you do after soaking the beans in water?

_____

_____

_____

3. How does the picture in Step 2 help you understand the text?

_____

_____

_____

4. What happens to the beans after 2–3 days?

_____

_____

Frog's Problem

Poor Frankie Frog! He has to read this speech on stage—but some of the *r*-blends have disappeared without a trace! Add an *r*-blend to each word to complete the speech. Some blends may be used more than once. We did one to get you started.

br	cr	dr	fr	gr	tr

__Gr__een frogs can croak.

Black _____ows can caw.

A train goes on _____acks.

A _____ape is a _____uit.

A _____ill makes holes.

Bread has a _____own _____ust.

These are all facts

you know you can _____ust!

A consonant blend is a group of 2 or more consonants in which each letter in the group makes its own sound. For example, the *pr* in *pretzel* is a consonant blend.

Peas in a Pod

Circle the number that completes each statement. We did the first one to get you started.

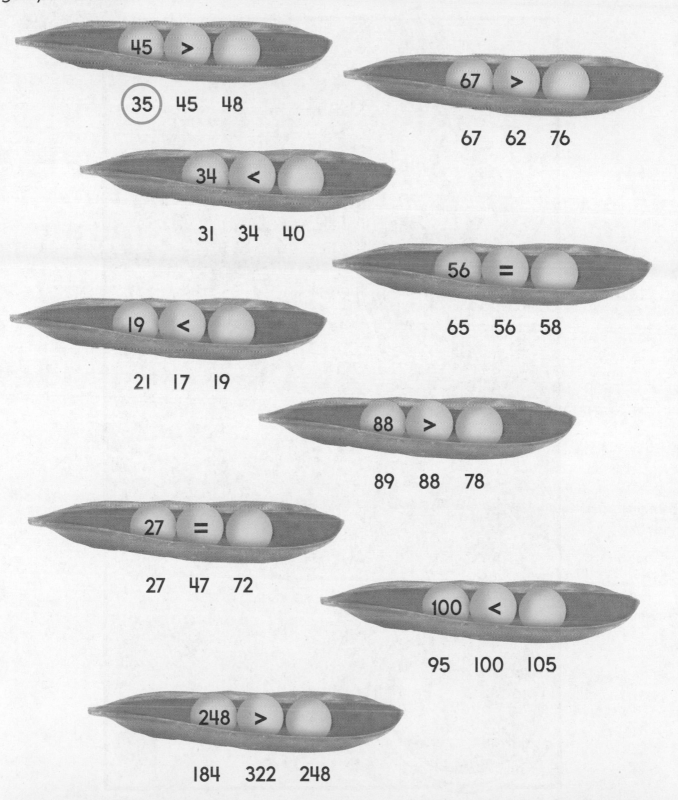

45 >

(35)   45   48

67 >

67   62   76

34 <

31   34   40

56 =

65   56   58

19 <

21   17   19

88 >

89   88   78

27 =

27   47   72

100 <

95   100   105

248 >

184   322   248

Count and Graph

Count to find out how many , and are in this picture.

Remember to cross off as you count.

Data: Organize, Represent, and Interpret Data

Complete the bar graph. Color one space for each
of the objects you counted.

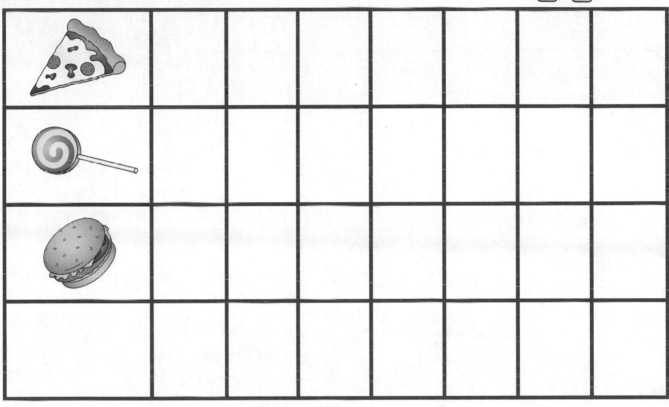

Use the graph to answer the questions.

1. How many lollipops are there?

2. Which 2 items appear the same number of times?

_____

3. How many fewer sandwiches are there than lollipops?

4. Count one other type of object in the picture on page 112. Add it to the

bar graph. How many boxes did you color to show how many?

Snug Space

Stan invited friends to visit on a stormy day. Write an **s**-blend to complete each word. Each blend will be used one time. Then find and circle the objects in the picture that match the words.

A consonant blend is a group of 2 or more consonants in which each letter in the group makes its own sound. For example, the *st* in *stamp* is a consonant blend.

| sc | sk | sl | sm | sn | sp | st | sw |

_____ate   _____ove   _____ippers

_____iles   _____oon   _____eaters

_____arves   _____owman

There's More in Store

The words in these two ladders are all spelled with **or** or **ore**. Use the clues to fill in the blanks. Each word is only one letter different from the word above it. We filled in the first one to get you started.

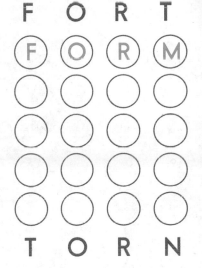

The vowel **o** changes when **r** comes after it. This sound can be spelled **or**, as in **for**, or **ore**, as in **store**.

F O R T

1. The shape of something   (F) (O) (R) (M)

2. You eat with this. ◯ ◯ ◯ ◯

3. A bottle stopper ◯ ◯ ◯ ◯

4. Middle of an apple ◯ ◯ ◯ ◯

5. Ripped a piece of paper ◯ ◯ ◯ ◯

T O R N

C H O R D

1. A kid's job around the house ◯ ◯ ◯ ◯ ◯

2. A beach ◯ ◯ ◯ ◯ ◯

3. Opposite of tall ◯ ◯ ◯ ◯ ◯

4. Nose noise made by a bull ◯ ◯ ◯ ◯ ◯

5. Noise made in sleep ◯ ◯ ◯ ◯ ◯

S T O R E

The **or** sound can also be spelled **oar**, as in **roar**; **oor**, as in **door**; or **our**, as in **four**.

Together as One

Pia, Mark, and Lori each used 2-dimensional shapes to make a picture. Their pictures are labeled 1, 2, and 3.

Which shapes did each child use? Label each shape on the table with the number of the matching picture. We did one to get you started.

Geometry: 2-D Composite Shapes

Match Them Up!

Draw a line from each group of shapes on the left to the matching composite shape on the right.

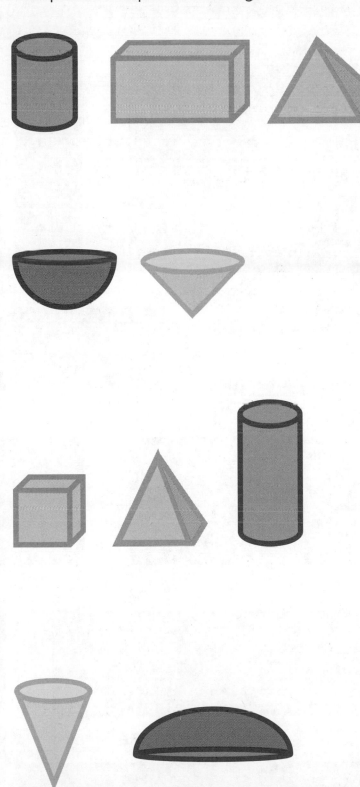

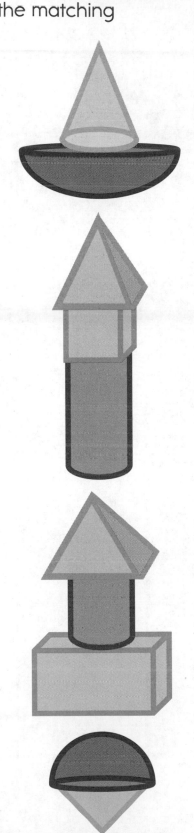

Koala Maze

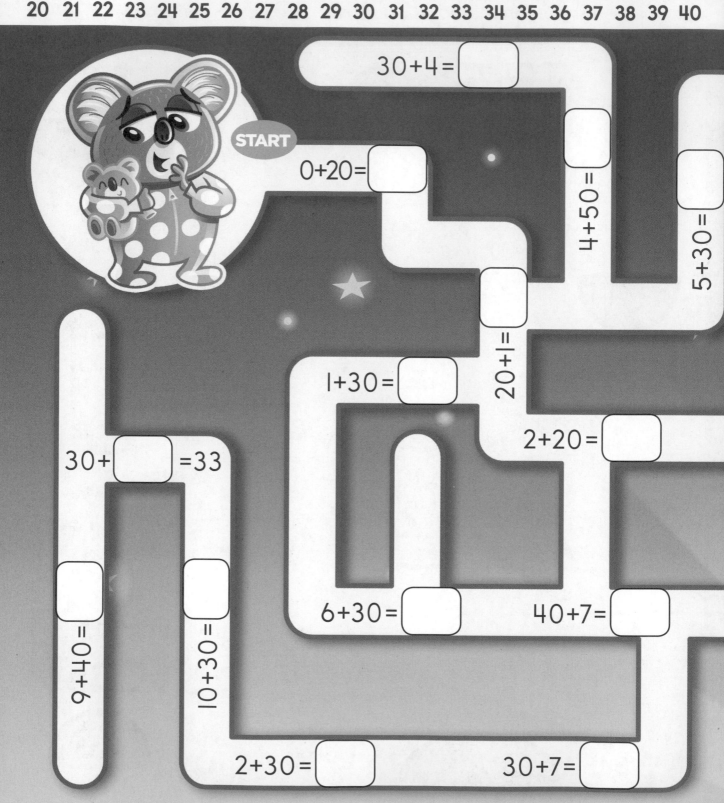

20 21 22 23 24 25 26 27 28 29 30 31 32 33 34 35 36 37 38 39 40

START

30 + 4 =

0 + 20 =

4 + 50 =

5 + 30 =

20 + 1 =

1 + 30 =

2 + 20 =

30 + ☐ = 33

6 + 30 =

40 + 7 =

9 + 40 =

10 + 30 =

2 + 30 =

30 + 7 =

Koalas can sleep up to 18 hours a day! Write the missing numbers to complete each problem. Use the number line if you need help. Then follow the numbers you wrote in order from 20 to 30 to help this koala reach her bed.

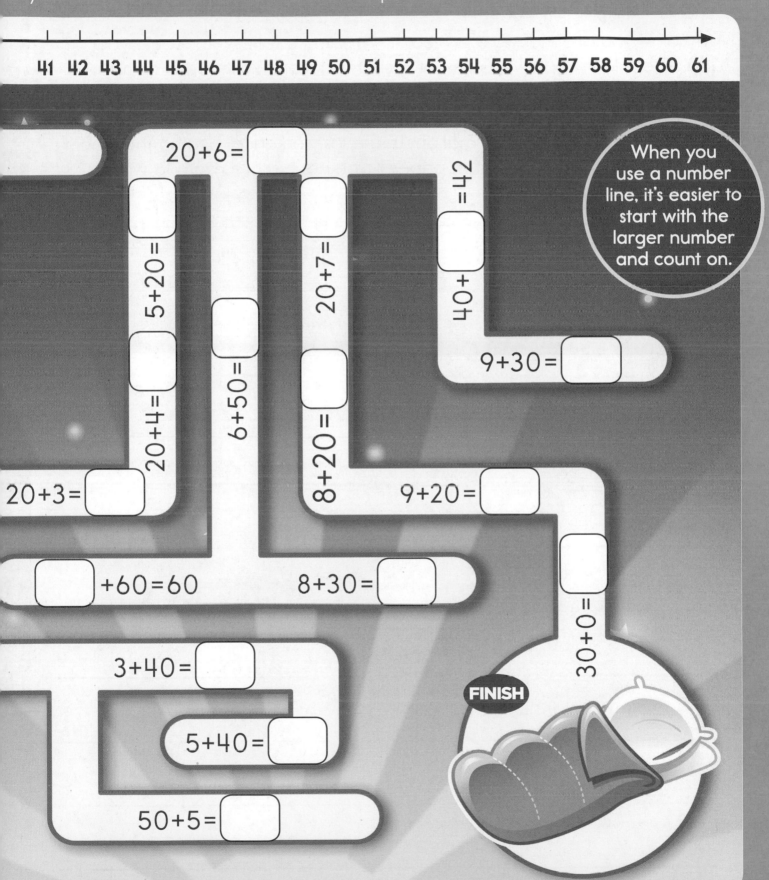

41 42 43 44 45 46 47 48 49 50 51 52 53 54 55 56 57 58 59 60 61

$20+6=$ ☐

$5+20=$ ☐

☐

$20+7=$ ☐

$=42$

$40+$ ☐

When you use a number line, it's easier to start with the larger number and count on.

$6+50=$ ☐

$9+30=$ ☐

$20+4=$ ☐

$8+20=$ ☐

$20+3=$ ☐

$9+20=$ ☐

☐ $+60=60$

$8+30=$ ☐

$30+0=$ ☐

$3+40=$ ☐

FINISH

$5+40=$ ☐

$50+5=$ ☐

119

Science Fair

Imagine you are making a project for a science fair. What would your topic be? How would you present the information? Write an informational text that tells about the science project you would make. In the first sentence, state the topic of the project. Then tell how you would research the topic and present information. In the last sentence, sum up the whole process. Use another sheet of paper if you need more room to write.

_____

_____

_____

_____

_____

_____

_____

_____

_____

_____

These kids are discovering lots of information at the school science fair!
Find and circle the 12 objects in this Hidden Pictures® puzzle.

cane

ruler

sailboat

slice of pizza

car

mitten

magnifying glass

banana

envelope

scarf

golf club

bird

BONUS!
Summer Craft Activity

Sunny-Day Clay

YOU WILL NEED:
- Baking soda
- Corn starch
- Water
- Food coloring

Give one of your clay creations to a friend to brighten his or her day.

1. With an adult's permission, pour 2 cups of baking soda, I cup of corn starch, and I 1/4 cups of water into a pot. Ask an adult to cook the mixture over medium heat, stirring until it looks like mashed potatoes.

2. Let the clay cool. Divide it into 4 pieces. Add food coloring and knead the clay until it is smooth.

Do you think the clay could dry without sun? Why or why not?

3. Make things with your clay.

4. Leave your creations in a sunny place to dry.

Lunch Dish

A digraph is a pair of consonants that make one sound. The *ch* sound is heard at the beginning of the word *chip*. The *sh* sound is heard at the beginning of the word *shell*.

What's for lunch? Write **ch** or **sh** to complete the words and find out what everybody likes to eat.

Charlie ____ooses to mun____ a sandwich with ____eese. He also has a fre____ pea____.

A ____icken pecks at seeds with her ____arp beak. Then she ____ares them with her ____icks.

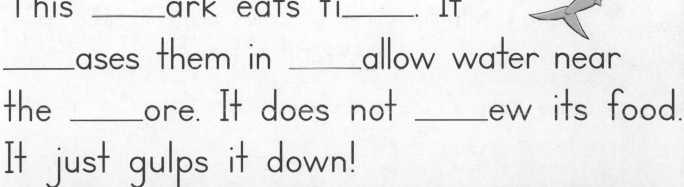

This ____ark eats fi____. It ____ases them in ____allow water near the ____ore. It does not ____ew its food. It just gulps it down!

Flowers for Sale

Bella and Ben Bee have a flower shop. Solve these word problems about the flowers they sold today.

Bella and Ben sold 12 orange daisies. They sold 8 more pink daisies than orange daisies. How many pink daisies did they sell?

$$\boxed{} + \boxed{} = \boxed{}$$

Bella and Ben sold 9 purple daisies to Glenda Grasshopper, 5 purple daisies to Lucy Ladybug, and 6 purple daisies to Simon Slug. How many purple daisies did they sell in all?

$$\boxed{} + \boxed{} + \boxed{} = \boxed{}$$

Bella and Ben had some white daisies. They sold 15 of them, and now they have 5 left. How many white daisies did they have to begin with?

$$\boxed{} - \boxed{} = \boxed{}$$

Bella and Ben sold 7 yellow daisies. They tied some of the daisies with blue ribbon and others with pink ribbon. How many daises could they have tied with each color? List each possible combination. We did one to get you started.

flowers with blue ribbon + flowers with pink ribbon = 7 daisies with ribbon

$$\boxed{1} + \boxed{6} = 7 \qquad \boxed{} + \boxed{} = 7 \qquad \boxed{} + \boxed{} = 7$$

$$\boxed{} + \boxed{} = 7 \qquad \boxed{} + \boxed{} = 7 \qquad \boxed{} + \boxed{} = 7$$

Operations: Addition and Subtraction Word Problems 0 to 20

Find and circle the **13** objects in this Hidden Pictures® puzzle.

spoon

scissors

pencil

ice-cream cone

crescent moon

teacup

BEES' FLOWERS

canoe

heart

fried egg

slice of pizza

football

piece of popcorn

magnifying glass

A Kite-Flying Day

Read the story. Then answer the questions on the next page.

Indi, Tex, and Niko were at the park with Niko's mom. They wanted to fly their kites.

Tex said, "If we hold our kites high, maybe the wind will catch them." But that didn't work.

"Maybe we should run really fast like this," said Indi. But that didn't work either.

"I think this may not be the best kite-flying day," said Niko's mom. "We might need to try again on a windier day."

As they headed for home, a strong gust of wind came along. It sent Tex's kite up, up, up! Niko and Indi saw Tex's kite flying high, so they quickly tried again.

"Look!" said Niko. "My kite is flying, too!"

"And so is mine!" said Indi.

"Hooray," cheered Niko's mom. "I guess it was the perfect kite-flying day after all."

1. How does Indi respond when Tex's kite does not fly?

_____

_____

2. Explain what the word **strong** means in this sentence: "As they headed for home, a strong gust of wind came along."

_____

_____

3. How do the children feel after their kites begin to fly? How do you know?

_____

_____

4. Which word best describes the children in the story?
    o shy   o bored   o determined

How Many Paper Clips?

Cheri is using paper clips to measure objects. Write the length of each object as a number of paper clips.

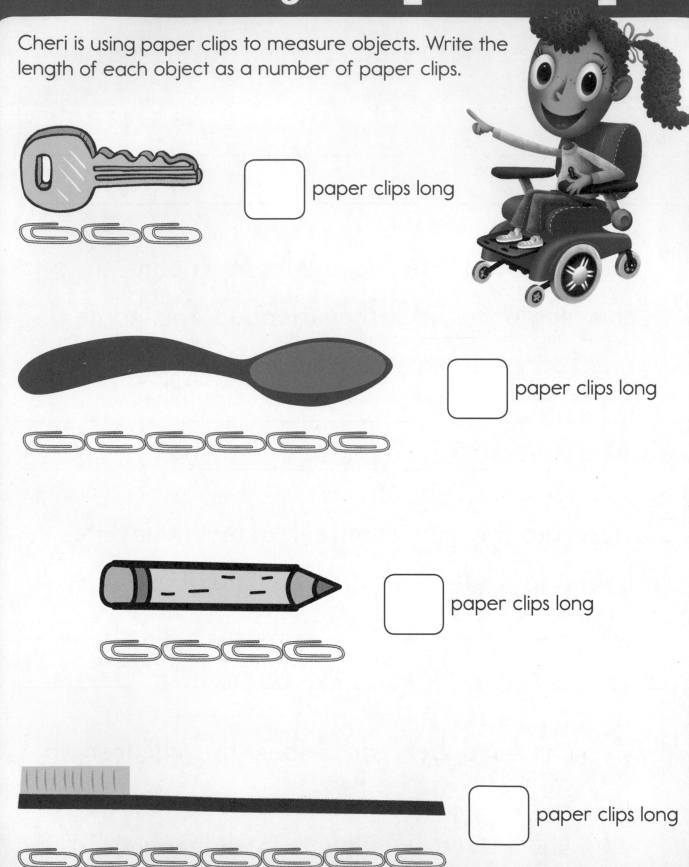

[ ] paper clips long

[ ] paper clips long

[ ] paper clips long

[ ] paper clips long

How Many Shoes?

Shane used his sneakers to measure his dresser. He walked his feet end over end, touching heel to toe. How many sneakers long is his dresser?

Shane's dresser is ⬚ shoes long.

Now it's your turn! Use a pair of your shoes to measure an object in your home. Draw the object and the number of shoes used to measure its length.

_____ is ⬚ shoes long.

Play Ball!

Use the hundred chart to add. Count on by tens.

1	2	3	4	5	6	7	8	9	10
11	12	13	14	15	16	17	18	19	20
21	22	23	24	25	26	27	28	29	30
31	32	33	34	35	36	37	38	39	40
41	42	43	44	45	46	47	48	49	50
51	52	53	54	55	56	57	58	59	60
61	62	63	64	65	66	67	68	69	70
71	72	73	74	75	76	77	78	79	80
81	82	83	84	85	86	87	88	89	90
91	92	93	94	95	96	97	98	99	100

$35+30=$ ☐

$73+20=$ ☐

$29+20=$ ☐

$30+57=$ ☐

$10+35=$ ☐

$51+10=$ ☐

$49+40=$ ☐

$15+60=$ ☐

$72+20=$ ☐

$50+45=$ ☐

79+20 = ☐

20+14 = ☐

10+84 = ☐

10+19 = ☐

67+30 = ☐

69+10 = ☐

64+10 = ☐

30+56 = ☐

50+12 = ☐

11+60 = ☐

15+20 = ☐

30+46 = ☐

Color each space that has a sum from the addition problems on these pages. You'll see a fun pair.

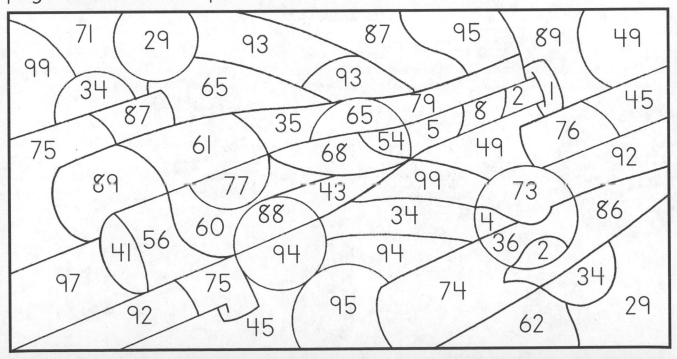

Half-and-Half

Draw a line in each shape to divide it in half.

Remember that halves are 2 equal parts.

Thomas ate 1 half of a cookie. Circle the cookie that shows 1 half missing.

Which 2 cookies are the same? Draw a line to match them.

Four in One

Draw lines in each shape to divide it into quarters.

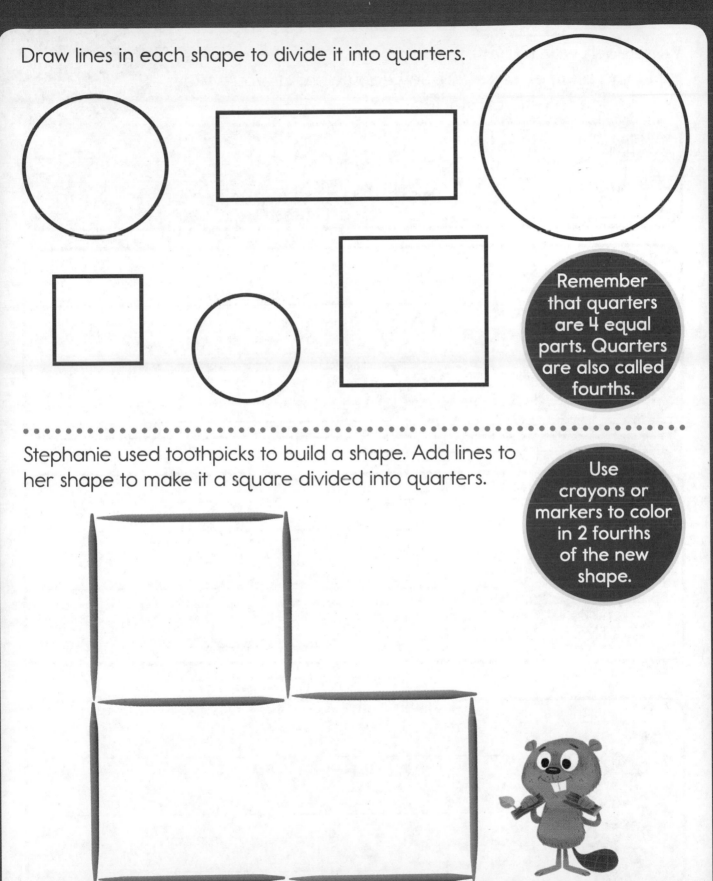

Remember that quarters are 4 equal parts. Quarters are also called <u>fourths</u>.

Stephanie used toothpicks to build a shape. Add lines to her shape to make it a square divided into quarters.

Use crayons or markers to color in 2 fourths of the new shape.

What's the Word?

When the vowel *e*, *i*, or *u* is followed by *r*, the vowel sound changes to include the *r* sound.

Write each word from the word bank in the box with the matching **er**, **ir**, or **ur** sound. Say each word as you write it. We did one to get you started.

bird   clerk   curls   dirt   ~~fern~~   fir   first
fur   germ   girl   her   hurt   nerve   nurse   turn

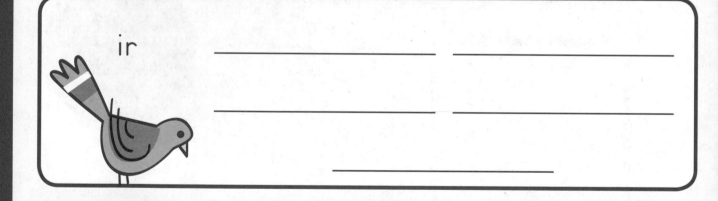

er   fern   _____   _____

_____   _____

_____

ir   _____   _____

_____   _____

_____

ur   _____   _____

_____   _____

_____

Planes and Trains

Compare the numbers above each plane. Use **> (greater than)** to write a statement that tells which number is greater. We did the first one to get you started.

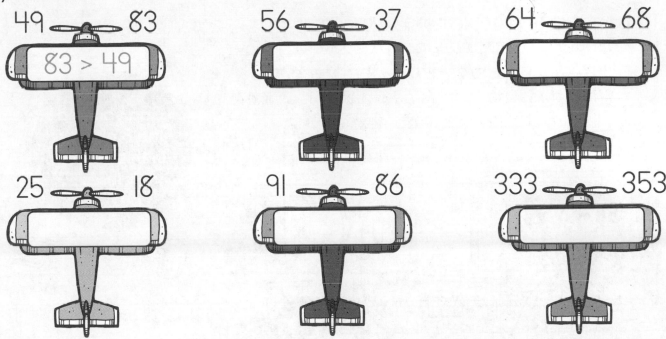

49 83   **83 > 49**

56 37

64 68

25 18

91 86

333 353

Compare the numbers above each train. Use **< (less than)** to write a statement that tells which number is less. We did the first one to get you started.

23 27   **23 < 27**

72 27

44 49

15 20

68 63

240 124

Tell a Story

Realistic fiction tells a story that is made up but could actually happen in real life. Look at the picture below. Use it to help you tell a realistic story about a brother and sister whose family adopts a puppy.

You may want to answer the following questions in your story:
- Where did the family go to choose a puppy?
- How many puppies did the family see?
- What does the family's new puppy look like?
- What might the family do next?

Can you find the 8 objects in this Hidden Pictures® puzzle?

cupcake

postage stamp

leaf

eyeglasses

lollipop

artist's brush

peanut

saucepan

Write sentences to tell your story about a family that adopts a puppy.

Use words such as *Then* and *after* to show the order of events. Add details that tell how the characters feel and what they are thinking. Give your story an ending that wraps up all the events.

_____

_____

_____

_____

_____

_____

_____

_____

_____

This and That

Fill in this grid with the *th* words and *ph* words below. Use the number of letters in each word as a clue to where it might fit. We did one to get you started.

4 Letters
MATH
THAT

5 Letters
GRAPH
MOUTH
PHONE
PHOTO
THICK
THUMB
TOOTH

6 Letters
GOPHER
MOTHER
THANKS
TROPHY

7 Letters
THIMBLE
THUNDER

8 Letters
ALPHABET
PHEASANT
~~THIRTEEN~~

Congratulations! You've completed **Chapter 8**—and this *Summer Big Fun Workbook*. **GREAT JOB!** Place your Chapter 8 sticker on the poster. Try this activity, and then fill out your Achievement Certificate.

BONUS!
Summer Science Activity

My Tree Journal

YOU WILL NEED:
• Camera   • Notebook or binder   • Paper
• Crayons or markers   • Glue or tape

1. Choose a nearby tree. With an adult's help, take a picture of the tree and put the photo in your notebook or binder.

2. Draw a picture of your tree for the cover of your journal.

3. Ask an adult to help you learn the name of the tree. You can find identification guides online or at your local public library.

4. Take photographs of your tree all year long. Add them to your journal.

How does your tree look in the summer? What happens in the fall? Keep track in your journal.

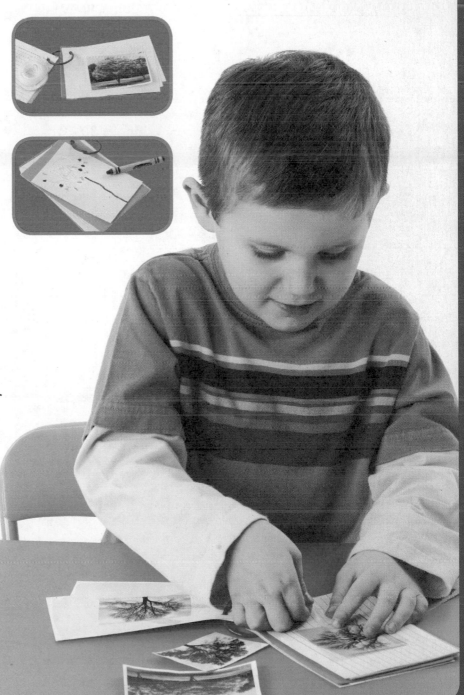

Answers

Page 9
Bird Watching

Pages 14–15
Baseball Riddles

What did the glove say to the baseball?

"CATCH YOU LATER!"

When do monkeys play baseball?

THEY PLAY IN APE-RIL.

Page 16
Sand Sounds

hat, glasses, castle, crab
You may have found others.

Pages 18–19
Campfire Equations

Freddy collected 16 logs.

Page 25
Sunshine Stumper

Why did the sun go to school?

TO GET BRIGHTER

Page 28
Yak with a Kayak

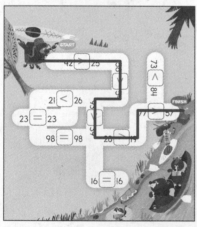

548 > 237

Pages 30–31
What's Missing?

7 + 3 = 10   10 + 3 = 13

6 + 6 = 12   12 + 5 = 17

8 + 3 = 11   15 = 9 + 6

7 + 9 = 16   20 = 10 + 10

4 + 5 = 9   19 + 0 = 19

14 - 0 = 14   18 - 9 = 9

18 - 9 = 9   20 - 3 = 17

12 - 2 = 10   5 = 8 - 3

15 - 10 = 5   0 = 20 - 20

18 - 7 = 11   15 = 19 - 4

Page 39
Beach Day!

Page 40
Coastal Colors

Pages 48–49
Climb to the Top

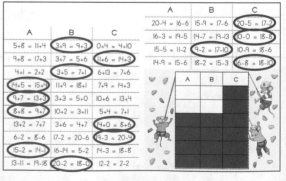

Mouse C will reach the top first.

Answers

Page 51
It's I Time

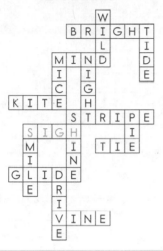

Page 53
A Dino and Digits

What was *T. rex*'s favorite number?

EIGHT (ATE)

Page 57
Time Out!

What do workers do in
a clock factory?

MAKE FACES

Page 61
Sandy's Strategy

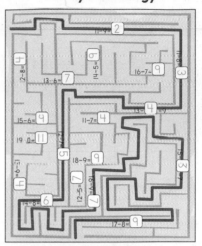

Pages 64–65
Coaster Maze

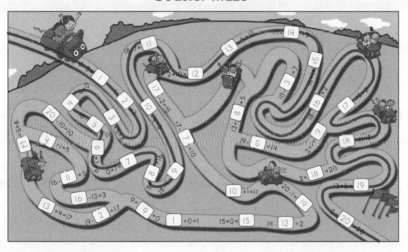

Page 67
Go, Gopher!

Page 80
Go, Team, Go!

Page 82
Shape Search

Page 85
Just for U

What is the difference between
a piano and a fish?

YOU CAN TUNE A PIANO,
BUT YOU CANNOT TUNE A FISH!

Answers

Page 89
From Y to Z!

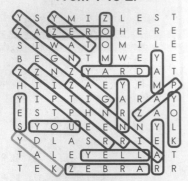

What is the longest word in the dictionary?

SMILES. THERE'S A MILE BETWEEN THE FIRST AND LAST LETTER!

Pages 91–92
At the Carnival

How many tickets does Yuri have?

35 tickets

Page 95
Cheese and Crackers

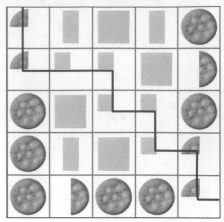

Page 98
Time for a Haircut

Page 100–101
Calculate This!

What did the student say to the calculator?

I AM COUNTING ON YOU.

Page 106
Down on the Farm

What is a cow's favorite school subject?

MOOSIC

Page 107
Down on the Farm

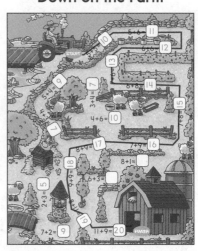

Page 115
There's More in Store

		F	O	R	T
1. The shape of something		F	O	R	M
2. You eat with this		F	O	R	K
3. A bottle stopper		C	O	R	K
4. Middle of an apple		C	O	R	E
5. Ripped a piece of paper		T	O	R	E
		T	O	R	N

		C	H	O	R	D
1. A kid's job around the house		C	H	O	R	E
2. A beach		S	H	O	R	E
3. Opposite of tall		S	H	O	R	T
4. Nose noise made by a bull		S	N	O	R	T
5. Noise made in sleep		S	N	O	R	E
		S	T	O	R	E

Pages 118–119
Koala Maze

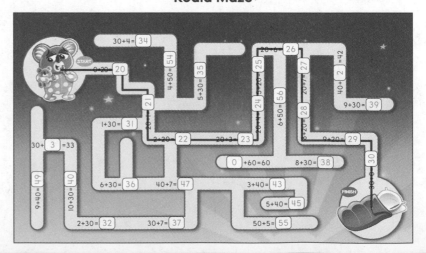

Answers

Page 121
Science Fair

Pages 124–125
Flowers for Sale

Bella and Ben Bee have a flower shop. Solve these word problems about the flowers they sold today.

Bella and Ben sold 12 orange daisies. They sold 8 more pink daisies than orange daisies. How many pink daisies did they sell?

$$12 + 8 = 20$$

Bella and Ben sold 9 purple daisies to Glenda Grasshopper, 5 purple daisies to Lucy Ladybug and 6 purple daisies to Simon Slug. How many purple daisies did they sell in all?

$$9 + 5 + 6 = 20$$

Bella and Ben had some white daisies. They sold 15 of them and now they have 5 left. How many white daisies did they have to begin with?

$$20 - 5 = 15$$

Bella and Ben sold 7 yellow daisies. They tied some of the daisies with blue ribbon and others with pink ribbon. How many daisies could they have tied with each color? List each possible combination. We did one to get you started.

flowers with blue ribbon + flowers with pink ribbon
= 7 daisies with ribbon

$$1 + 6 = 7 \qquad 3 + 4 = 7 \qquad 5 + 2 = 7$$
$$2 + 5 = 7 \qquad 4 + 3 = 7 \qquad 6 + 1 = 7$$

Pages 130–131
Play Ball!

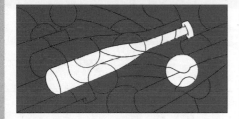

Page 136
Tell a Story

Page 138
This and That

Summer Big Fun Adventure Progress Poster

Congratulations!

_____
(your name)

worked hard
and finished the

Summer
Big Fun Workbook

Summer Stickers

When you finish a chapter, place that chapter's sticker on the matching sign on the poster. Finish all 8 chapters and place all 8 stickers to complete your **Summer Big Fun Adventure!**

Use these sun stickers to mark each spot on the poster where you find a hidden magnifying glass.

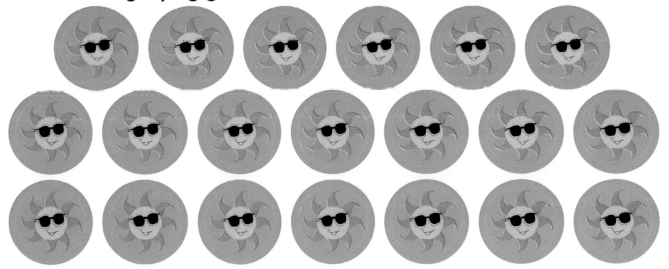

Place these emoji stickers on your favorite pages in this book—or use them to decorate a notebook or share with friends!